The Hemmings Book of

MUSTANGS

ISBN 0-917808-79-7
Library of Congress Card Number: 2001093619

One of a series of Hemmings Collector-Car Books. Other books in the series include:
The Hemmings Book of Buicks; The Hemmings Motor News Book of Cadillacs; The Hemmings Book of Postwar
Chevrolets; The Hemmings Motor News Book of Corvettes; The Hemmings Motor News Book of Chrysler
Performance Cars; The Hemmings Book of Prewar Fords; The Hemmings Motor News Book of Postwar Fords; The
Hemmings Motor News Book of Hudsons; The Hemmings Book of Oldsmobiles The Hemmings Motor News Book of
Packards; The Hemmings Motor News Book of Pontiacs; The Hemmings Motor News Book of Studebakers.

Hemmings Motor News
Collector Car Publications and Marketplaces
1-800-CAR-HERE (227-4373)
www.hemmings.com

The Hemmings Book of

MUSTANGS

Editor-In-Chief
Terry Ehrich

Editor
Richard A. Lentinello

Designer
Nancy Bianco

Cover photo by Vince Wright: 1965 Mustang GT 2+2

This book compiles driveReports which have appeared in Hemmings Motor News' Special Interest Autos magazine (SIA) over the past 30 years. The editors at Hemmings Motor News express their gratitude to the following writers, photographers, and artists who made this book possible through their many fine contributions to Special Interest Autos magazine:

Arch Brown	Michael Lamm
Dave Brown	Vince Manocchi
Dave Emanuel	Alex Meredith
Jerry Heasley	Rick Mitchell
M. Park Hunter	Roy Query
Bud Juneau	Russ von Sauers
John F. Katz	Vince Wright

We are also grateful to Dave Brownell, Michael Lamm, and Rich Taylor, the editors under whose guidance these driveReports were written and published. We also thank the following organizations, which have graciously contributed photographs to Special Interest Autos magazine and this book:

Detroit Public Library
Ford Motor Company
Motor Trend magazine
Road & Track magazine
Sports Car Club of America

CONTENTS

Special Interest Autos (SIA) magazine's back issues are referred to in this book by issue number. If in stock, copies may be purchased directly from Hemmings Motor News at 800-227-4373 or at www.hemmings.com.

First Mustang:
Trendsetter of the 1960s

the 1964/65 Mustang stands out, in my opinion, as the milestone car of the 1960s. No other automobile of that decade exerted greater influence on the industry. The Mustang caused the entire ponycar rage. At least six additional domestic ponycars plus two imported ones owe (or owed) their existence to the Mustang: Camaro, Cougar, Firebird, Javelin, Challenger, Barracuda (actually the Barracuda preceded the Mustang by two weeks, but it did come in answer to it), Capri, and Toyota Celica. The Mustang fostered the 1960s trend to longer hoods and shorter decks.

This, then, is the story of the first Mustang's conception and development. In 1961, the car was simply one man's hunch—a raw, formless, unnamed notion. By 1963 it had become a firm and tactically brilliant idea. By Apr. 1964 when Ford introduced it, the Mustang immediately became the most important and imitated car in the world. I believe we'll see the first-series Mustang go down in automotive history not just as a milestone but also as a very collectable, likable car.

by Michael Lamm, *Editor*

tAKE A COURSE in college economics and you'll likely study the Ford Mustang—not as a car but as a marketing case history. The Mustang shows one very right way to merchandise anything big and important, be it a car, color TV, suburban subdivision, or a political candidate. The Ford Motor Co. made no mistakes on the way to the Mustang, and that's a rare thing in the car business. In fact, the Mustang's rightness helped erase the Edsel boo-boo, a miscalculation that left Ford with a $250 million egg on its face.

In 1968, Ford published a resource paper on the Mustang, aimed specifically at college business and economics students. Its purpose: to show the world that right decisions, right design, and right timing have their roots in a balanced mix of careful market research and gut hunches.

The man who supplied most of the gut hunches and who wrote that resource paper—figuratively if not literally—was Lido Anthony (Lee) Iacocca, the son of a rags-to-riches, immigrant Italian who made it big in car rentals and real estate.

Lee's father, Nicola, came to this country from his home in southern Italy, aged 12. As a teenager, he scraped together enough cash to buy a second-hand Model T, which he rented out from time to time to acquaintances in and around Allentown, Pa. Within eight years, Nicola's rental business blossomed to 33 cars, most of them Fords. Soon the elder Iacocca expanded and branched out into real estate. The family's holdings reached a net worth of over a million dollars even before the Depression—a fortune they managed to keep largely intact through the hard times.

Quoth TIME Magazine in a cover story on Lee Iacocca at the first Mustang's introduction (Apr. 17, 1964): "Lee Iacocca never wavered from early youth in his desire to go into the auto business—with Ford. For him, it was something like wanting to join the priesthood. 'I suppose it was partly because my father had always been greatly interested in automobiles,' he says, 'and because I was influenced by family friends who were Ford dealers.'"

Lee Iacocca breezed through high school with excellent grades, received his bachelor's degree from Lehigh University, took a master's in mechanical engineering from Princeton (on scholarship), whizzed through an 18-month Ford marketing course in half that time, and found himself afterward with an offer to become a Ford transmission engineer. Not for him, he said, and instead he took a job in a tiny Ford sales outpost in Pennsylvania. He did exceedingly well, of course, and whisked his way up the various regional Ford ladders until, in 1956, he came to the attention of Robert McNamara, who at that time was Ford Div. general manager. McNamara borrowed a sales scheme that Iacocca had dreamed up in Washington and applied it to the whole country: the "$56 a month for a 1956 Ford" plan. It worked nationwide, and McNamara said later that it helped Ford sell an additional 72,000 1956 Fords.

From there, promotions came thick and fast. The cigar-puffing, hawk-faced Iacocca boosted the sale of any truck and car Ford he touched, even though Ford often didn't build them the way Iacocca would have liked.

Mustang's ornamental gas cap launched a trend. Convertible doesn't blast passengers at speed.

Ponycar revolution started here. Original Mustang combined sporty good looks with low price and long option list

He wrote in his little black book that by age 35 he intended to become a Ford vice president. Iacocca's black book—in fact a whole raft of black books—had already become dinner conversation all over Dearborn. Iacocca had earlier run into flak from underlings who resented so young a man telling them what to do. So he passed out little black books, asking members of his staff to put down what they expected to accomplish over the next few years and in what order of importance. Every three months, then, he graded them against these self-imposed goals. When some of the older men groused, he told them, "Get with it. You're being observed. Guys who don't get with it don't play on the club after a while." One staffer snuffled, "He really knows how to whipsaw his men with that notebook."

Iacocca's 35th birthday came and went without a vice presidency. Later he told a NEWSWEEK reporter that he was so disappointed that he thought to himself, "Hell, that's the end." But 18 days later, Henry Ford II called him into his office and asked if he'd like to be a vice president of Ford Div. One year after that, in Nov. 1960, Iacocca had taken McNamara's place as Ford Div. general manager. (McNamara soon became Pres. Kennedy's defense secretary.)

the Mustang was one of those entries in Iacocca's personal black book. It sprang from a hunch that there must be a market out there looking for a car.

People were still writing in, asking Ford to *please* revive the old 2-seater Thunderbird. They missed its "personal" personality. Meanwhile Chevrolet had lucked into an unexpected mini-bonanza with the bucket-seated Monza. The Monza series began to account for 76% of Corvair sales soon after its Mar. 1961 debut. Then, too, imported sports cars like Jaguar, MG, Triumph, and Austin-Healey were selling

a brisk 80,000 units a year despite fairly high prices. Also relatively expensive but much admired and talked-about were the Corvette and Avanti.

If that sort of flashiness and performance could be stuffed into an inexpensive car for the masses—no doubt about it: The market would gobble it up.

So here was the glint of a trend, and Lee Iacocca sat there and scribbled it down in his black book. He was thinking of the sort of car he himself might want—a young man's car. This was in early 1961, even before the Monza came out, and the idea was still pretty hazy. The car didn't have a name, of course, nor was it defined as a 2-seater, 4-seater, front- or rear- or mid-engined, metal or fiberglass. All those decisions came later.

For the moment, Iacocca was still trying to bring Ford Div. back from the rather lack-luster image it had gotten under McNamara. Not that McNamara had been a poor administrator: financially he left Ford Div. (which accounted for 80% of Ford Motor Co. sales) in beautiful shape. But McNamara reacted to the 1958 Detroit excesses by putting Fords into what amounted to plain, brown wrappers. TIME commented that McNamara's cars were, "... like McNamara himself, [with] rimless glasses and hair parted in the middle."

So following DeLorean's lead at Pontiac, Iacocca, when he took over as Ford general manager in 1960, started to spruce up the various Ford lines. He got there too late to do much about the 1961-62 models, which were already crystalized, but he jazzed up the 1963½s considerably. It was Iacocca who dropped the first V-8 into the Falcon, added the Falcon hardtop, put fastback roofs on some Ford lines, and who plunged Ford back into auto racing in a big way. After Iacocca talked Henry II into re-entering NASCAR, Fords dominated all the big southern tracks. Soon Ford had also won

Ford Motor Co.

Lee Iacocca and the Mustang: mutual makers.

Even without handling package, Mustang corners gracefully. Beefier suspension cost $31.30 extra. Mustangs distinguished themselves as rally cars.

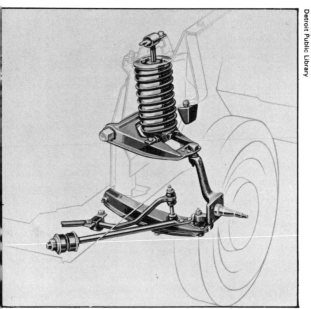

Ford suspension engineers took best qualities of Fairlane/Comet springing and applied them to Mustang.

Buckets and carpeting are standard, with front bench optional. Falcon-like instruments stand out as one of the few items that really don't blend with the car's sporting nature.

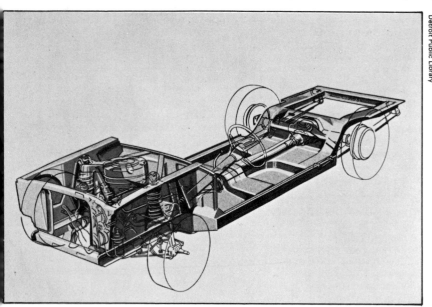

Early mechanical prototypes had too stiff a platform, which caused noise and vibration. Mustang convertible used same platform as coupe but of a heavier metal.

To keep costs down, Joe Oros and his design team hung very little frill on Mustang but did keep "scoop" behind sweep.

Power top cost $54 extra (above), and most owners ordered it. One casualty of long hood, short deck is trunk space. It's very tight.

Falcon aircleaner and radiator tank had to be flattened to fit under Mustang hood. Basic engine was the 170-cid 6, with 260- and 289-cid V-8s optional.

Mustang Production by Body Style

	coupe	fastback	convertible	total
1964	92,708	- - -	28,833	121,541
1965	409,260	77,079	73,112	559,451
1966	499,751	35,698	72,119	607,568
1967	356,271	71,042	44,808	472,121
1968	249,447	42,581	25,376	317,404
1969	150,640	134,438	14,746	299,824
1970	96,150	86,904	7,673	190,727
1971	83,102	60,455	6,121	149,678
1972	75,395	43,297	6,401	125,093
1973	76,754	46,260	11,853	134,867
1974*	229,007	103,177	- - -	332,184

*1974 figure is for Mustang II. **Source**: Ford Motor Co.

First Mustang

Sebring, won Indy, and nearly won Le Mans. It was all part of Iacocca's "thinking young."

Which brings us back to the Mustang. Iacocca first broached the topic at a meeting of the Fairlane Group, a loose 8-man committee of top Ford brass plus members of the division's ad agency. The Fairlane Group got its name by meeting once a week at the Fairlane Inn Motel on Michigan Av. in Dearborn. The group decided that this idea of Iacocca's might be worth pursuing. They tentatively called it Project T-5. (Much later, production 1965 Mustangs were sold in Germany under the designation T-5.)

Two additional groups now became involved in T-5: market research, under the direction of Ford Marketing manager Chase Morsey Jr., plus a team of young Ford engineers and designers headed by Donald N. Frey, who at that time was Iacocca's product planning manager. (Today Frey is board chairman of Bell & Howell in Chicago.)

The idea of bringing in market research was, of course, to either back up or disprove Iacocca's hunch. Product planning's role was to come up with a car to fill the market void, if indeed there was one.

Morsey's research analysts were keenly aware of the risk of another Edsel. Ford Motor Co. couldn't afford that much egg again, which meant that if the market didn't exist, or if it were marginal (as was the Monza market, even with sports cars tossed in), forget it. But market research came up with some very encouraging conclusions, to wit:

1) Members of the WW-II baby boom were just starting to turn car-buying age. Further, young people aged 15-29 would increase in number by about 40% between 1960 and 1970, while 30-39-year-olds would actually decrease by 9%.

2) Morsey expected that young buyers, 18-34, would account for more than half the increase in new-car sales projected from 1960 through 1970.

3) Research showed that car styling in the 1960s would have to reflect the preferences and tastes of young people, not the older generations. Young buyers had clear ideas about styling and performance. The Ford corporate study concluded that, "...36% of all persons under 25 liked the 'four on the floor' feature. Among those over 25, only 9% wanted to shift gears. Bucket seats were a favorite feature among 35% of young people, as against 13% in the older groups. Some 42% preferred bucket seats for the first dates...."

4) Buyers were becoming more educated, more sophisticated, more willing to spend cash for "image extensions."

5) Families had more money, and those with incomes of $10,000 and up were expected to rise 156% between 1960 and 1975. Thus more were willing to buy second (and third and fourth) cars. Women and teenagers were demanding and getting cars of their own.

So research confirmed that the market was definitely out there: an affluent, young group that was big enough to support a new kind of car—something distinctive and sporty and not too expensive. The question remained, though: Precisely what should the T-5 become?

here's where Don Frey's product planning group stepped in. Frey huddled with Gene Bordinat, Ford's design vice president, and of course it just happened ("") that Bordinat's corporate projects studio had a number of small, bucket-seated, sporty prototypes on hand. Actually this was no coincidence, because all car manufacturers' styling studios produce a

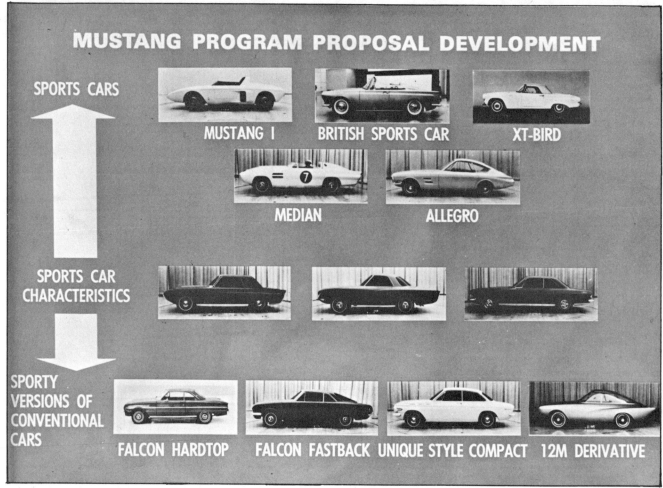

MUSTANG PROGRAM PROPOSAL DEVELOPMENT

SPORTS CARS

MUSTANG I   BRITISH SPORTS CAR   XT-BIRD

MEDIAN   ALLEGRO

SPORTS CAR CHARACTERISTICS

SPORTY VERSIONS OF CONVENTIONAL CARS

FALCON HARDTOP   FALCON FASTBACK   UNIQUE STYLE COMPACT   12M DERIVATIVE

Corporate proposal, drawn up after final Mustang decision, shows the many alternatives considered—from 2-seaters through Cardinal and Falcon.

First Mustang

steady flow of such ideas cars—there always seem to be some kicking around. In early 1961, the cars that surfaced were called things like Mina, Median, and one had the label "open sports car."

The Fairlane Group reviewed these cars and asked that one—dubbed "median sports car," a 4-seater—be worked up into coupe and convertible body styles. The median sports car captured, they felt, some of the personal flavor of the 2-seater Thunderbirds. In addition to the straight 4-place package, the median sports car was mocked up as a 2-seater, as a 2+2 with jumpseats, and as a 2+2 with a cramped set of rear buckets.

The median sports car evolved into a second generation called Avventura. There were 12 clays in the Avventura series, one of which became the Allegro X-Car, shown publicly in Aug. 1963. All told, there were 13 Allegros, each differing slightly in dimensions and interior packaging.

Meanwhile off to one side came a tiny 2-seater called the Mustang I—a lithe, low, rocket-shaped aluminum job with a V-4 engine amidship. The V-4 was borrowed from the Ford Cardinal project, which had been set for production in this country but was suddenly bumped by pricing problems plus Iacocca's ideas for a sportier new car. The Cardinal eventually became the Ford Taunus 12-M, and

one of these days we'll do an article on it—it's interesting. Anyway, the Mustang I stirred great rushes of adrenalin among Ford designers and engineers, and Ford finally turned it loose at Watkins Glen in the fall of 1962. The fans couldn't get enough of it. Dan Gurney drove it and raved. Would the Watkins Glen crowd buy one? Sure they would.

Iacocca: "All the buffs said, 'Hey, what a car! It'll be the best car ever built.' But when I looked at the guys saying it—the offbeat crowd, the real buffs—I said, 'That's sure not the car we want to build, because it can't be a volume car. It's too far out.'" Exit Mustang I.

By this time the Avventura/Allegro series was getting a little worked-over and stale, so Bordinat, Frey, Iacocca, Henry II, and the others involved decided to start over with a new series of clays. This was in Aug. 1962—around Aug. 2. The basic package was firmed up, and four studios were now invited to compete in the design. The package called for: price $2500, weight 2500 pounds, four seats, overall length not more than 180 inches, bucket seats, floorshift, and mostly Falcon mechanical components. Personality: sporty, personal, tight, and then here's where Ford tossed in the marketing brainstorm, probably the key to the whole thing—a long, long option list that would let owners tailor the car toward economy, luxury, or performance.

With the package roughly defined, the four competing styling studios were turned loose. These were the Ford Div. studio, Lincoln-Mercury studio, corporate projects, and advanced

styling. All, of course, worked under Gene Bordinat, and he gave them an Aug. 16 deadline to come up with suitable scale clays—two weeks.

The four studios submitted a total of seven clays, and on Aug. 16 these were arranged side by side out in the Ford Design Center courtyard. Of the seven, one leapt out from the rest. "It was the only one in the courtyard that seemed to be moving," said Iacocca later, and Henry Ford II agreed with his choice.

This was the model created by the Ford Div. studio under Joe Oros, now executive director of Ford and Lincoln-Mercury design. Members of the Oros team included Gail Halderman, Ford car manager, and David Ash, executive designer. Oros had gathered his people together at the beginning of the assignment, and before anyone even put pencil to paper, they talked the project over at length. "We said what we would and wouldn't do. We didn't want the car to look like any other car; it had to be unique." They talked so much, in fact, that when they finally got down to drawing the car, that part took only three days.

The result was a clay that looked very nearly like the production Mustang, but without a front bumper. Oros called it the Cougar, and that name was later changed to Torino (or Turino in some citings) and finally, confusingly, to Mustang II. Oros painted the clay white so it *would* leap out at the showing.

Market research, meanwhile, was still taking pulses. Ford conducted no fewer than 14 separate surveys. One queried only Monza owners. Another compared seating preferences

This aluminum roadster, with Taunus/Cardinal V-4 amidship, was first to carry Mustang name. Car buffs loved it, but Iacocca saw it wasn't for the masses.

With market research pointing toward 4-seater, Ford designers began claying this sort of car—a natural extension of compacts.

Attempts were made to incorporate Thunderbird & Falcon sheetmetal in early Mustang sketches. Cougar II (r) came closer but was too complicated.

Allegro (left) was changed a dozen times before designers gave up. Allegro II(center) remained showcar. Artisan carves Mustang out of mahogany.

for the VW, Monza, and the proposed Mustang (none by name). Another showed that among people under 25, a car's looks ranked as the primary selling point, with price second. Yet another concluded that young buyers preferred 4-seaters to 2-seaters by a margin of 16 to one.

Perhaps the most interesting experiment involved 52 couples—husbands and wives with pre-teen children. Each couple was led into a big room that had the prototypal Mustang 4-seater standing in the center. Interviewers asked the couple how much they thought the car would cost. Answers were inevitably several thousand dollars above the $2500 target price. Asked whether they thought they might be interested in buying this car, all of them said no. But then, told that the car would sell for $2500 or less, husbands and wives went back for a second look, and without exception they

began to find reasons why the car really might be practical for them after all.

On Sept. 10, 1962 the Oros/Ford "Cougar" was approved and orders came down to productionize it. At this point, Ford engineering got involved, which was unusual, because normally engineering is called into a project much earlier. Said Jack J. Prendergast, Ford's executive engineer for light vehicles, "Styling kept the engineers out too long, but even so engineering and styling worked together very smoothly." Except for the normal compromises, all went well. Engineering bent over backward, in fact, to keep the Mustang's styling integrity intact.

The Mustang became 90% a body engineering job, because the basic chassis, engine, suspension, and driveline components were all

carried over from the Falcon and Fairlane. Overall length was identical to the 1964 Falcon: 181.6 inches. Wheelbase was cut 1.5 inches to 108. Some initial thought had been given to sharing Falcon sheetmetal with the Mustang, but that idea didn't last long.

According to Ford studio manager Gail Halderman, "We had to bend something like 78 Ford Motor Co. in-house standards or rules in order to build this car." Halderman is referring to a rulebook used by Ford designers at that time. It listed certain specific do's and don't's; for example, no radical tuck-under as in the Mustang's rear fenders; greater bumper-to-sheetmetal clearance than conceived; no die-cast bezel in front of the headlights; and much less roll-under to the front bumper pan.

Where engineering couldn't fit structural pieces under styling's outlines (as in the front

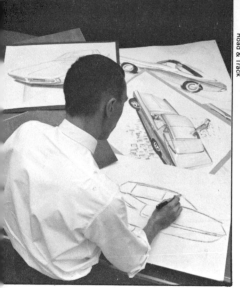

After Allegro, Ford studios started afresh, competed to decide final Mustang design.

Clay modelers will cover wooden body buck to outlines spelled out by stylists.

Ford Div. studio under Joe Oros won competition with this design. Iacocca took racer Graham Hill for a spin in it (inset). Hill found rear leg room cramped, so Iacocca added an inch in production.

This was one of the seven competing clays viewed in Design Center courtyard on Aug. 16, 1962.

By Dec. '62, Mustang looked like this, but a Cougar graced grille. Cougar name, of course, was held over for Mercury's version of the Mustang, which shared all the first ponycar's basics.

Options: *Mustang's Other Success Secret*

Standard equipment in the 1965 Mustang included the 170-cid Falcon 6, 3-speed manual transmission, full wheelcovers, padded dash, bucket seats, carpeting, and floorshift. Beyond that, though, the Mustang offered a tremendous variety of options to help personalize and custom-tailor the car. Here's a smattering.

-260-cid, 164-bhp V-8	$116.00
-289-cid, 210-bhp V-8	181.70
-289-cid, 225-bhp V-8	162.00
-289-cid, 271-bhp V-8	442.60
-Cruise-O-Matic w/6	179.80
-Cruise-O-Matic w/V-8	189.60
-4-speed manual trans w/6	115.90
-4-speed manual trans w/V-8	188.00
-Limited-slip differential	42.50
-Rally-Pac (tach & clock)	70.80
-Special handling package	31.30
-14-in. wheels & whitewalls	41.00
-14-in. styled steel wheels	122.30
-Power brakes	43.20
-Disc brakes (late 1965)	58.00
-Power steering	86.30
-Power top for convertible	54.10
-Air conditioning	283.20
-Console	51.50
-Bench front seat	24.95
-Deluxe steering wheel	32.20
-Vinyl roof covering	75.80
-Rocker panel molding	16.10
-Pushbutton radio w/antenna	58.50
-Tinted windshield & glass	30.90
-Knockoff wheelcovers	18.20
-Simulated wire wheels (covers)	45.80
-Visibility group (mirrors, wipers)	36.60
-Accent group (stripes, moldings)	27.70
-5-dial instrument panel	109.40
-GT group (disc brakes, trim)	168.60

specifications

Russ von Sauers, The Graphic Automobile Studio

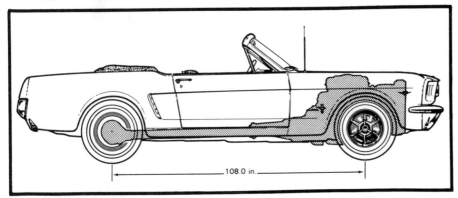

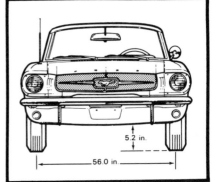

108.0 in.

5.2 in.

56.0 in.

1965 Ford Mustang 76-A 4-passenger convertible coupe

Price when new .... $2368 f.o.b. Dearborn (1964).
Options .... 289/210-bhp V-8, automatic transmission, power steering, power top, radio, whitewall tires.

ENGINE

Type .... Ohv V-8, cast-iron block, water-cooled, 4 mains full-pressure lubrication.
Bore & stroke .... 4.00 x 2.87 in.
Displacement ..... 289.0 cid.
Max. bhp @ rpm ... 210 @ 4400.
Max. torque @ rpm . 300 @ 2800.
Compression ratio .. 8.9:1.
Induction system ... Single 4-bbl. carburetor, mechanical fuel pump.
Exhaust system .... Cast-iron manifolds, crossover pipe, single muffler.
Electrical system .... 12-volt battery/coil.

CLUTCH

Type .... None

TRANSMISSION

Type .... Cruise-O-Matic 3-speed automatic torque converter with planetary gears.
Ratios: 1st ...... 2.46:1.
2nd ...... 1.46:1.
3rd ...... 1.00:1.
Reverse .... 2.20:1.

DIFFERENTIAL

Type .... Hypoid, Hotchkiss drive.

Ratio .... 3.00:1.
Drive axles .... Semi-floating.

STEERING

Type .... Recirculating ball & nut, linkage power assist.
Turns lock to lock .... 3.7.
Ratio .... 21.7:1.
Turn circle .... 38.0 ft.

BRAKES

Type .... 4-wheel hydraulic drums, internal expanding.
Drum diameter ..... 10.0 in.
Total swept area .... 251.3 sq. in.

CHASSIS & BODY

Frame .... Unitized body/frame.
Body construction ... All steel.
Body style .... 2-door, 4-passenger convertible coupe.

SUSPENSION

Front .... Independent SLA, high-mounted coil springs, ball joints, anti-roll bar, tubular hydraulic shock absorbers.
Rear .... 1-piece axle, semi-elliptic leaf springs, tubular shock absorbers.
Tires .... 6.50 x 14 2-ply tubeless whitewalls.
Wheels .... Pressed steel centers, drop-center rims, lug-bolted to brake drums.

WEIGHTS & MEASURES

Wheelbase .... 108.0 in.
Overall length ..... 181.6 in.
Overall height ..... 51.0 in.
Overall width ...... 68.2 in.
Front tread .... 56.0 in.
Rear tread .... 56.0 in.
Ground clearance .... 5.2 in.
Curb weight .... 2742 lb.

CAPACITIES

Crankcase .... 4 qt.
Cooling system ...... 14 qt.
Fuel tank .... 16 gal.

FUEL CONSUMPTION

Best .... 21-24 mpg.
Average .... 16-19 mpg.

PERFORMANCE from Road & Track,
May 1964 test of 210-bhp with 4-speed stick.

0-30 mph .... 3.6 sec.
0-40 mph .... 5.1 sec.
0-50 mph .... 6.9 sec.
0-60 mph .... 8.9 sec.
0-70 mph .... 11.6 sec.
0-80 mph .... 14.9 sec.
Standing ¼ mile .... 17.0 sec. and 85 mph.
Top speed (av.) ...... n.a.

First Mustang

pan, which left no room for bumper bracing), they revised the car's lines as little as possible. With the many different engines and horsepowers contemplated, it was essential to have a rigid base. Prendergast recalled, "The platform-type frame, evolved from previous light-car experience, was designed to be really in the middle. All the various chassis components were attached to the underside, and all the body components were installed topside."

Heavy box-section siderails with five welded-in crossmembers formed the base. The convertible used heavier-gauge steel and got extra reinforcements in the rocker areas. The first coupes actually had frames so stiff that they resonated vibrations, so these were softened slightly.

Prendergast pointed out that at that time they had learned from previous mistakes in the Falcon and Comet—things done much better in the Fairlane and Mustang. Suspension components drew heavily from Falcon Sprint/ Comet Caliente/Fairlane experience. To get the hoodline down; running changes were made in the 1964 Falcon, Comet, and Fairlane long

before the Mustang arrived: a lowering of air-cleaner height and a countersinking of the radiator filler cap. Thus all mechanical parts were in production and catalogued by parts numbers several months before the Mustang debuted.

Meanwhile there was still the problem of naming the new car. Different Ford departments had given the car working titles—Allegro, Avventura, Cougar, Turino, Torino, and of course Mustang. Henry Ford II liked "T-Bird II" or "Thunderbird II." Iacocca had no strong preferences.

To research the topic, John Conley from Ford's ad agency went down to the Detroit Public Library to see what he could come up with. It was Conley who earlier had combed lists of birds to discover Falcon and lists of Indian talismans to find Thunderbird. This time he leafed through words having to do with horses.

Conley produced a long list, which included Colt, Bronco, Maverick, and again Mustang. Mustang had been used on at least two show-cars, and after very little debate, it was chosen. In many ways it was a natural. It embodied power, speed, independence, and freedom; it connoted cowboys, prairies, movie adventures, the romantic West; it was easy to spell and easy to remember. As one Ford adman put it: "It

had the excitement of the wide-open spaces, and it was American as all hell."

target date for introduction was Apr. 17, 1964, the day the New York Worlds Fair opened. As unveiled, the Mustang created a national sensation, and more about that in a moment.

The car's base price stood comfortably below Iacocca's initial $2500 target. It was $2368 f.o.b. Dearborn for the coupe. That included full wheelcovers, buckets, floorshift, padded dash, and carpeting. More important, customers could choose among four engines, six transmissions, three suspension packages, three brake systems, three wheels sizes, plus multitudinous comfort, luxury, performance, and styling options. It was no trick at all to optionize a Mustang to double its base price, and many buyers did just that.

The Mustang hit with a bang like no other car of the 1960s. FoMoCo publicists saw to that as they spread the word with an enthusiasm that matched the public's natural curiosity.

On Mar. 11, 1964, Henry Ford II's nephew, Walter Buhl Ford III, 20, happened (again"") to be driving a pre-production, black Mustang convertible to lunch in downtown Detroit. Fred

First Mustang

Olmsted, auto editor of the *Detroit Free Press*, spotted it in a parking lot and called photographer Ray Glonka to hurry on over to snap a shot. He did, and the picture was picked up by *Newsweek* and a number of other publications. It was the first glimpse of a Mustang fed to a national audience, and if anything, it heightened the public desire to see the car in the flesh.

Time had a deal with Ford to be allowed to take pictures of the Mustang as it was being developed. Photographer J. Edward Bailey had been with Oros and Bordinat almost since the beginning of the "Cougar" clay, but *Time* promised not to publish anything on the Mustang until introduction day. *Time* kept its promise, but despite hopes for an exclusive on the Mustang, both *Time* and *Newsweek* ran simultaneous cover stories on Iacocca and his baby's birth. It was a rare trick that Ford publicists had pulled. Concurrently *Life, Look, Esquire, US News & World Report*, the *Wall Street Journal*, and most business and automotive journals carried big articles on the Mustang.

On the evening of April 16, Ford bought the 9:00 p.m. time slot on all three major TV networks, so 29 million viewers got to see the Mustang's unveiling without leaving their living rooms. The next morning 2,600 major newspapers carried announcement ads (and articles) for the Mustang. Some 150 auto editors had been invited to the World's Fair as Ford's guests, and after sumptuous wining and dining, were allowed (the next day) to drive Mustangs from New York to Detroit. "These were virtually handbuilt cars," recalls one Ford information officer, "and anything could have happened. Some of the reporters hotdogged these cars the whole way, and we were just praying they wouldn't crash or fall apart. Luckily everyone made it, but it was pure luck." The luck paid off in glowing reports the following week.

Mustangs were put on display in airport terminals, Holiday Inn lobbies, and naturally, dealer showrooms across the country. Everywhere, the car's price stood out boldly. Crowd reaction was tremendous. A San Francisco trucker stared so hard at a Mustang in a dealer's showroom window that he drove right in through the glass. A Chicago dealer had to lock his doors to keep more people from crowding in and crushing each other and his cars. A Pittsburgh dealer made the mistake of hoisting his only Mustang up on his lube rack, and the crowds pressed in so thick and fast that he couldn't get the car down until suppertime. At one eastern dealership, 15 customers craved the same new Mustang, so the dealer finally auctioned it off. The winning bidder insisted on sleeping in his car so he'd be sure it wasn't sold out from under him before his check cleared the next morning.

Dealers simply couldn't get Mustangs fast enough. All the early ones were sold at or above retail, with very unliberal trade-in allowances. Ford had set the first sales projection at 100,000 cars. This was long before introduction. As the World's Fair approached, Iacocca upped the quantity to 240,000 and added assembly facilities at Ford's San Jose

> *"It took only four months to sell 100,000 Mustangs, and by the end of the 1965 model year, a total of 680,992 cars had been sold."*

plant. It took only four months to sell 100,000 Mustangs, and by the end of the 1965 model year (April 1964 through December 1965), a total of 680,992 cars had been sold. This represented an all-time industry record for first-year sales. By March 1966, the millionth Mustang rolled off the line. It's a record made even more impressive by the fact that the Mustang had only two body styles, coupe and convertible, until September 1964, when the fastback was added.

road & Track wrote in May 1964: "For the Mustang is definitely a sports car, on par in most respects with such undisputed types as the MG-B, Triumph TR-4, or Sunbeam Alpine. It is also more than a sports car by virtue of a more elaborate design concept: The Mustang buyer tailors his car to his special requirements from a lengthy option list. It can be made into a luxurious Baby Thunderbird; it can be ordered ready to race; it can be a comfortable *gran turismo* car; it can be tailor-made for suburban housewives; and it is easily set up for the...drags."

Dan Gurney, writing in *Popular Science* about his 271-bhp Mustang with 4-speed: "This car will run the rubber off a Triumph or an MG. It has the feel of a 2+2 Ferrari. So what *is* a sports car?" His car had a top speed of 123 mph and consistently beat a similarly equipped Corvette in acceleration runs up to and including the quarter mile.

The 1964 1/2 Mustang we borrowed for this driveReport belongs to Charles and Georgia Herring of Stockton, California. It has the 289-c.i.d., 210-bhp V-8, Cruise-O-Matic, and power steering—a common and practical combination. The car now shows 98,000 miles on the clock, but it feels as tight and lively as ever.

I've driven quite a few early Mustangs, and they've always impressed me as being an ideal size, not too big and not too small. The car fits. Ford certainly hit the "personal" nail dead center, and that's where the later Mustangs— the 1969-73 models—missed. They were all too big.

There are a few minor things that bother me about this car. The gauge cluster, for instance, is one item that's out of keeping with the rest of the Mustang. Too, I find the pinch handle for the shift selector bothersome to use. A button on top would be better. The early drum brakes leave a lot to be desired. They're Falcon 9-inchers for the 6, 10-inchers with the V-8, and discs didn't arrive until 1965.

Ride feels good, and for $32 extra, the handling package was a bargain. Not enough people bought it. Even so, this car handles well. You can set the rear adrift in a hard, fast turn, and with proper throttle it just hangs there.

Rear seating is a bit cramped, but I don't expect anyone bought a new Mustang figuring he'd get a lot of hip room. Nor rear knee room. Nor trunk space. These are all very tight, and to my thinking they accounted for the eventual fall of all ponycars. The rage began on the basis of looks and ended (wups, it hasn't quite ended yet) on the basis of impracticality. Nice as they are, ponycars really aren't very practical.

The second-generation Mustang II has quite a set of shoes to fill if it expects to be half the car its daddy was. But I don't believe another milestone like that original Mustang is likely to come along soon—not until one person, be it Mr. Iacocca or someone else, gets that fiery passion stoked up and sustains it. That's a rare thing. ◌

Our thanks to Lee A. Iacocca, Gene Bordinat, Jack Prendergast, Walt Murphy, Cara Benson, Michael W.R. Davis, Glen Willardson, and Gail Halderman of Ford Motor Co., Dearborn; and Burt Weaver, Oakland, California.

Ford Mustang Hardtop

A PRODUCT OF Ford MOTOR COMPANY

New Ford Mustang

$2368* f.o.b. Detroit

This is the car you never expected from Detroit. Mustang is so distinctively beautiful it has received the Tiffany Award for Excellence in American Design... the first time an automobile has been honored with the Tiffany Gold Medal.

You can own the Mustang hardtop for a suggested retail price of just $2,368—f.o.b. Detroit.
*This does not include destination charges from Detroit, options, state and local taxes and fees, if any. Whitewall tires are $33.90 extra.

Every Mustang includes these luxury features unavailable—or available only at extra cost—in most other cars: bucket seats; wall-to-wall carpeting; all-vinyl upholstery; padded instrument panel; and full wheel covers. Also standard: floor-shift; courtesy lights; sports steering wheel; front arm rests; a 170 cu. in. Six, and much more.

That's the Mustang hardtop. With its four-passenger roominess and surprisingly spacious trunk, it will be an ideal car for many families. Yet Mustang is designed to be designed by you. For instance, the trip to the supermarket can be a lot more fun when you add convenience options like power brakes or steering, Cruise-O-Matic transmission, push-button radio, 260 cu. in. V-8.

Or, you can design Mustang to suit your special taste for elegance with such luxury refinements as: air conditioning; vinyl-covered roof; full-length console; accent paint-stripe, and convertible with power top.

If you're looking for action, Mustang's the place to find it, with a 289 cu. in. V-8; 4-speed fully synchronized transmission; Rally-Pac (tachometer and clock) and other exciting options.

For an authentic scale model of the new Ford Mustang, send $1.00 to Mustang Offer, Department A-1, P.O. Box 35, Troy, Michigan. (Offer ends July 31, 1964)

TRY <u>TOTAL</u> PERFORMANCE
FOR A CHANGE!

FORD

Mustang · Falcon · Fairlane · Ford · Thunderbird

RIDE WALT DISNEY'S MAGIC SKYWAY AT THE FORD MOTOR COMPANY'S WONDER ROTUNDA, NEW YORK WORLD'S FAIR

1955 Thunderbird vs. 1965 Mustang

The Story of a Bird and a Horse

Originally published in Special Interest Autos #145, Jan.-Feb. 1995

by Arch Brown
photos by Bud Juneau

Top left: *T-Bird carries sporty theme to the road with attractive wire wheel covers. Comparison Mustang uses optional Styled Steel wheels.* **Above:** *Thunderbird's distinctive headlamp eyebrows became elongated coves on the Mustang.* **Below:** *T-Bird's parking lamps were prominent above the bumper; Mustang's are nearly hidden in sheet metal below.*

WHEN it comes to sporty personal cars, Ford appears to have pioneered the concept. Twice, in fact: in 1955 with the original Thunderbird, and just short of a decade later with the Mustang.

The story begins with Lewis D. Crusoe, general manager of the Ford Division. During the fall of 1951, Crusoe was traveling in France. That October, accompanied by George Walker, the styling consultant who had been largely responsible for the design of the 1949 Ford (see *SIA* #139), he attended the Paris Salon. He found himself enchanted by some of the two-passenger sports cars that were on display there: the Jaguar, the Pegaso, and the recently revived Bugatti. "Why don't we have something like that?" Crusoe reportedly asked of Walker. And Walker replied, not altogether accurately, that his staff was already at work on just such an automobile.

By this time it was an open secret that Chevrolet was developing a fiberglass-bodied two-seater, the car that would come to market in 1953 as the Corvette. Supposedly, reports of this project aroused little interest among members of the Ford high command, although Henry Ford II made no secret of his determination to meet General Motors head-on in every market segment. In any event, Franklin Quick Hershey, Ford's talented young styling director, believed that the men in the front office could be convinced; so he and a young associate named Bill Boyer had quietly

begun to develop some renderings.

Inevitably, Hershey learned of Lewis Crusoe's enthusiastic reaction to the two-place cars he had seen at the Paris show; and this gave new impetus to his and Boyer's efforts. Nor was the message lost upon George Walker. The upshot was that both the Hershey and Walker teams got cracking, and several proposals were developed.

The result of all this was the 1955 Thunderbird, and even today there are conflicting claims as to who was really responsible for its design. Some say that Bob Maguire, head of the Ford passenger car studio, played a major role.

Others credit a Ford stylist named Damon Wood with much of the work. But it's pretty clear that it was Frank Hershey and Bill Boyer who were chiefly responsible.

When the Thunderbird was introduced, on September 9, 1954, the company did not call it a "sports" car. It was far too luxurious for that, featuring such amenities as roll-up windows and a full roster of power options. Rather, it was billed, much more accurately, as a "personal" car. Surprisingly, however, some prominent members of the automotive press *did* refer to it as a "sports" car. *Motor Trend*'s Walt Woron, for example,

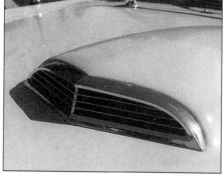

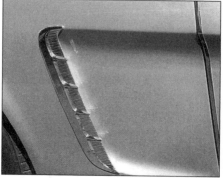

Above and below: T-Bird's classy removable hardtop gave car an extra dimension of style and usefulness. With Mustang you could have a convertible or hardtop, but not both. *Right:* Hoodscoops were all the rage as a styling device in the fifties. Mustang, however, uses faux rear brake scoops.

SIA comparisonReport

declared that "although the Ford Motor Co. is the first one to deny it, they have a *sports car* (italics Woron's) in the Thunderbird, and it's a good one." Even the often critical Tom McCahill, writing in *Mechanix Illustrated*, called the 'Bird "a full-blown sports car as far as I am concerned."

At least, there was no denying that the Thunderbird was a performer, thanks to its use of the '55 Mercury's 292-c.i.d. Y-block V-8. As teamed with the standard three-speed manual transmission (with or without the optional overdrive), this engine developed 193 horsepower; while in combination with the Ford-O-Matic

transmission, due to an increase in the compression ratio from 8.1:1 to 8.5:1, it was rated at 198.

Whatever it was — sports car, personal car, little limousine — the public loved it. Ford's corporate bean-counters had projected annual sales of 10,000 units, but the T-Bird did much better than that. Production for the 1955 model year came to 16,155 units, compared to only 700 Corvettes built that season by Chevrolet.

Even so, from a sales standpoint the little T-Bird was handicapped by its limited seating capacity, and almost from the day of its introduction plans were being developed for a larger, four-passenger version, on the premise that a broader market could be reached if the Thunderbird had a back seat. The larg-

er model was introduced on February 13, 1958, following an extended 1957 season which proved to be the "Little Bird's" parting shot.

Of course, the pundits were correct about the saleability of the four-place T-Bird. In the face of the severe 1958 recession, and despite its abbreviated production year, sales rose by 77 percent that season. And by the following year, with the economy back on track, Thunderbird sales reached 67,456 units, substantially more than the three-year (1955-57) grand total for the two-passenger model.

But still, no Thunderbird since that time has ever had quite the charm of the "Little Birds" of 1955-57.

If the original Thunderbird was a success — and it obviously was — how is one to describe the first-generation Mustang's impact on the market? This time, the initial projection called for sales of 75,000 Mustangs during the first year of production. But in view of the intense public interest stirred by the car, the target was raised to 200,000, even before the Mustang went on display. That figure was eventually doubled, far outstripping the capacity of the Dearborn factory; and additional assembly points were established at San Jose, California, and Metuchen, New Jersey. In the end, 418,812 new Mustangs were delivered during the first twelve months of production.

The demographics were clearly favorable toward an automobile of this type. Members of the wartime "baby boom" generation were just commencing to enter the automobile market in substantial numbers. On the whole, these young people were better educated and more prosperous than their parents had

1955 Thunderbird Options (partial list)

Ford-O-Matic transmission	$178
Overdrive transmission	$110
Power steering	$91
Power brakes	$32
Power seat (4-way)	$64
Power windows	$102
Soft top (in lieu of fiberglass top)	$75
Soft top (in addition to fiberglass top)	$290
Radio	$99
Heater	$71
White sidewall tires	$27

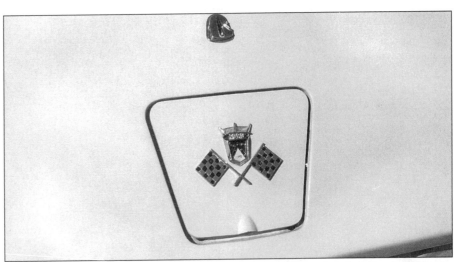

Left and above: Thunderbird can be gassed up with trunk open or shut. Cap is hidden by appropriately decorated flap. Mustang, **below,** leaves cap exposed as a decorative element.

been, which augered well for the future of the automobile industry. Furthermore, as America moved to the suburbs there was a rapid growth in the number of two-car families. Women were becoming an increasingly important factor in the automobile market, and typically, the ladies preferred small, nimble cars — as well as stylish ones.

At the same time, it should be noted that there was plenty of opposition within the company to the idea of putting money into the development of a small, sporty automobile. It was early 1962 when consideration was first given to what was to become the Mustang project. Scarcely more than two years had passed since the demise of the ill-starred Edsel, and Ford executives were still licking their wounds following that debacle. Careful market research had, after all, pointed to a rousing success for the Edsel.

It was Lido Anthony "Lee" Iacocca, general manager since 1960 of the Ford Division, who really pushed for the development of a stylish, sporty small car — a four-passenger job, this time. Iacocca wasn't a stylist, but he did have in mind the long hood/short deck concept that would mark the Mustang as a style leader. Evidently that idea came from the original Thunderbird, which Iacocca had long admired.

Eighteen different clay models were produced by Ford's styling department during the first seven months of 1962. Some were attractive, even exciting, but none seemed exactly right. The twin goals of the as yet unnamed project were, first, to keep the price under $2,500, and second, to have the car ready by April 1964, in time for the opening of the New York World's Fair.

Time was running out; so styling director Gene Bordinat staged a contest among the corporation's three major styling studios: Ford, Lincoln-Mercury and Corporate Projects, the latter being the company's advanced styling operation.

In the end, the winning proposal was that of Dave Ash, assistant to Ford studio head Joe Oros. Tentatively known as the Cougar, Ash's proposal was surprisingly close to the final version, the car that became the Mustang.

There still were plenty of doubters. Ford President Arjay Miller worried that the Mustang would steal sales from the Falcon and the Fairlane. Which, in fact, it did, but it also generated a lot of new business — "conquest" sales, in the language of the trade. The bean-counters

1964½ (early 1965) Mustang Options (partial list)

164-horsepower, 260-c.i.d. V-8 engine	$116.00
210-horsepower, 289-c.i.d. V-8 engine	$181.70
Cruise-O-Matic transmission (6-cyl.)	$179.80
Cruise-O-Matic transmission (8-cyl.)	$189.60
4-speed manual transmission (6-cyl.)	$115.90
4-speed manual transmission (210-horsepower V-8)	$188.00
Power steering	$86.30
Power brakes	$43.20
Power top (convertible)	$54.10
Air conditioner	$283.20
Pushbutton radio (with antenna)	$58.50
Tinted glass (throughout)	$30.90
Console, full-length (with Cruise-O-Matic)	$51.50
Rocker panel molding	$16.10
White sidewall tires (7.00/13)	$33.90
Rally-Pac clock and tachometer	$70.80
Visors, padded	$5.70
Windshield washer with 2-speed wipers	$20.10

This page: In our test the older car actually felt like it handled the corners better than its sibling. *Facing page:* T-Bird's taillamp design followed that of regular "55 Fords. Mustang's treatment is unique to the marque.

SIA comparisonReport

questioned whether the company could afford the tooling costs, at a time when a completely restyled full-sized Ford was also under development.

On September 10, 1962, Iacocca was given the green light. Forty million dollars was earmarked for development and tooling, an incredibly low figure, feasible only because a lot of Falcon and Fairlane components could be employed. And of course, if the April 1964 introduction date was to become a reality, the customary three-year startup time would need to be cut in half.

As everyone knows by now, the Mustang did make its scheduled introduction date. Both *Newsweek* and *Time* featured the smart little car on their cov-

ers, an unprecedented salute for an automobile. Then, to the delight of everyone involved, the Mustang became the first motorcar ever to be given the Tiffany Award for Excellence in American Design. No amount of money could have bought that kind of publicity. The Mustang was even selected to pace the 1964 Indy 500, and *Time* ventured to predict that it "seems destined to be a sort of Model A of sports cars."

The base price for the hardtop was set at $2,368, well within the target figure. Even the convertible cost only $2,614. Standard equipment included such luxury touches as vinyl bucket seats, sports steering wheel, carpeting, padded dash, courtesy lights and full wheel covers. But it soon became apparent that the typical buyer wanted more than the base model. Most of the new Mustangs left the showroom equipped with close to a thousand dollars worth of high-

profit options. Ford had hit upon a veritable bonanza.

There were two base powerplants, both borrowed from the contemporary Falcon: a 170-c.i.d., four-bearing, 101-horsepower six, and a 260-cubic-inch V-8, rated at 164 bhp. For those who wanted a little extra sauce, an extra $65.70 over the price of the standard V-8 would buy a 210-horsepower, four-barrel version of the larger, 289-c.i.d. version.

The standard transmission was a three-speed manual gearbox with a floor-mounted lever, but both the Cruise-O-Matic and a four-speed manual were offered at extra cost. Other popular options included power steering, power brakes, a power top for the convertible, air conditioner, radio, and a long list of attractive trim items.

From the beginning, the Mustang was advertised as a 1965 model. But on October 1, 1964, when the balance of the 1965 Ford line was introduced, a slightly revised edition appeared, along with an additional body type, a sleek fastback. Chief among the modifications in these "true" 1965 models was a pair of larger standard engines. Replacing the Falcon Six was a new 200-c.i.d., 120-horsepower, seven-bearing mill, a much more competent performer than its predecessor. And in lieu of the 260, V-8 buyers got a 289-c.i.d., 200 horsepower engine. Optional versions of the 289 were rated at 225 and 271 horsepower. All of which, of course, only enhanced the Mustang's appeal!

Driving Impressions

We have been unable to learn very much about the early history of our fea-

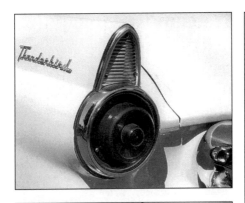

Specifications: 1955 Thunderbird vs. 1965 Mustang

	1955 Thunderbird	1965 Mustang
Base price	$2,944	$2,614
Engine	Ohv V-8	Ohv V-8
Bore x stroke	3.75 x 3.30 inches	3.80 x 2.875 inches
Displacement	291.6 cubic inches	260.8 cubic inches
Compression ratio	8.10:1	8.40:1
Horsepower @ rpm	193 @ 4,400 rpm	164 @ 4,400 rpm
Torque @ rpm	280 @ 2,600	268 @ 2,200
Taxable horsepower	45	46.20
Valve lifters	Hydraulic	Hydraulic
Main bearings	5	5
Carburetor	1 four-bbl	1 two-bbl
Exhaust system	Dual	Dual (orig. single)
Electrical system	12-volt (orig. 6-volt)	12-volt
Transmission	3-speed manual with overdrive	Cruise-O-Matic 3-speed with torque converter
Control lever	Floor	Console
Speeds	3	3
Ratios	2.32/1.48/1.00	2.46/1.46/1.00
Overdrive ratio	0.700:1	----------
Converter ratio at stall	----------	2.02
Rear axle	Hypoid	Hypoid
Ratio	3.73:1	2.80:1
Drive axles	Semi-floating	Semi-floating
Steering	Power assisted	Power assisted
Turns, lock-to-lock	3.5	3.75
Ratio, gear/overall	20.1/20.1	16.0/21.7
Turning diameter	38 feet, 6 inches	38 feet, 11 inches
Brakes	Hydraulic, drum	Hydraulic, drum
Drum diameter	11 inches	10 inches
Effective area	169.7 square inches	127.8 square inches
Construction	Body-on-frame	All steel unitized
Frame	Central X-member, box-section side rails, 4 crossmembers	All steel unitized body and frame
Body construction	All steel	All steel
Body type	2-passenger convertible coupe	4-passenger convertible coupe
Front suspension	Independent, coil springs, ball joints	Independent, coil springs, ball joints
Rear suspension	Rigid axle, longitudinal leaf springs	Rigid axle, longitudinal leaf springs
Shock absorbers	Tubular, direct-acting	Direct-acting telescopic
Wheels	Steel disc	Steel disc
Tires	6.70/15 originally, now 7.10/15	6.50/14 originally, now 195-75/R14
Wheelbase	102 inches	108 inches
Overall length	175.3 inches	181.6 inches
Overall width	70.3 inches	68.2 inches
Overall height	50.2 inches	51.5 inches
Front track	56 inches	56 inches
Rear track	56 inches	56 inches
Min. road clearance	5.9 inches	5.6 inches
Shipping weight	2,988 pounds	2,615 pounds
Crankcase capacity	5 quarts (with filter)	5 quarts (with filter)
Cooling system capacity	20 quarts (with heater)	15 quarts (with heater)
Fuel tank	17.5 gallons	16 gallons
Transmission	3 lb. + 1.5 o.d.	17 pints
Rear axle	3 lb.	4.5 lb.
Stroke/bore ratio	0.88:1	0.76:1
Horsepower/c.i.d.	.662	.629
Weight per horsepower	15.5 pounds	15.9 pounds
Weight per c.i.d.	10.2	10.0
PSI (brakes)	17.6	20.5
Performance*: 0-30 mph	3.6 seconds	4.2 seconds
0-50 mph	7.3 seconds	9.4 seconds
0-60 mph	9.6 seconds	12.3 seconds
Top speed	130 mph (est)	97.5 mph

* (from road tests by Mechanix Illustrated)

tured Thunderbird, except that it was originally a Chicago car. Miraculously, it escaped the rust that is the scourge of so many Midwest collectors. It did not, however, escape sheet metal damage, of which it had sustained plenty, both front and rear.

The 'Bird logged about 165,000 miles during its first two decades of service. At that point — 1975 — it was acquired by a California collector who, evidently intending to restore the car, pulled the engine and sent it to a machine shop for rebuilding. From there the car went to a body shop for some metal work and a new paint job, after which it was returned to its owner in pieces. For reasons that remain obscure, it sat in the owner's garage, still disassembled, until 1982, when it was acquired by its present owner, Brent Hokanson, of Fairfield, California.

It took Brent about a year to reassemble the Thunderbird, partly because of the time it took to find replacements for a number of missing or non-authentic trim parts. The previous owner had overhauled the front end, and Brent went through the transmission and brakes, and converted the electrics to a twelve-volt system. He also added a 1957-style carburetor and air cleaner and a Mallory dual point distributor, and substituted an AM/FM radio with tape deck for the original AM unit.

The 'Bird is Brent's only passenger car, though he owns a modern pickup. He has covered about 15,000 miles in it since the restoration was completed, including trips through the Pacific Northwest, to Reno, and down the San Joaquin Valley. He reports that it is a marvelous highway cruiser, fast, comfortable, and easy to handle.

SIA comparisonReport

Thunderbird's steel hardtop requires a bit of muscle and a second pair of hands to remove efficiently, while the ponycar's top can be transformed at the touch of a button.

To be absolutely fair in making this comparison, both machines should be fitted with similar drivetrains. This is not the case with our comparisonReport cars, for our Thunderbird is equipped with a manual shift and overdrive, while the Mustang has a Cruise-O-Matic transmission. Walt Woron, evaluating a 1955 Thunderbird for *Motor Trend*, found acceleration with the stick shift "just about even with a Ford-O-Matic 'Bird." On the other hand, *Mechanix Illustrated*'s Tom McCahill road-tested two Thunderbirds, one fitted with the stick-and-overdrive combination, the other with the automatic. In his experience, the stick shift car was a second and a half faster than the Ford-O-Matic in the zero-to-sixty run, and he estimated that the difference in top speed to be close to 15 miles an hour.

(Incidentally, upon completing his road tests of the two Thunderbirds, McCahill ordered one for himself — equipped, like Brent Hokanson's car, with the manual shift and overdrive.)

The clutch in Brent's T-Bird is smooth, and requires only moderate pressure. I found, however, that shifting the transmission into low is a bit tricky. Gears will clash unless the driver touches second gear before engaging low. Of course, first gear is not synchronized; but even so, it should engage without complaint if the shift isn't made too rapidly.

Acceleration was, as I fully expected,

How Quickly Time Passes!

Nearly ten years elapsed between the debut of the original Thunderbird and that of the first Mustang. The world had changed in many ways, yet so much remained the same:

In 1955, Dwight Eisenhower was in the White House. Ten years later the occupant was Lyndon Johnson, signaling a major shift in the balance of political power.

Among the major events of 1955 were the perfection, by Dr. Jonas Salk, of the polio vaccine. In labor relations, the AFL and the CIO merged, ending a 20-year separation. And Marian Anderson made her operatic debut at New York's Metropolitan Opera House, the first African American to become a regular member of the company. Sixteen years earlier, because of her race, she had been barred by the Daughters of the American Revolution from giving a concert at Constitution Hall.

In his 1965 State of the Union address, President Johnson outlined his program for a "Great Society," and seven months later Medicare was signed into law. Riots in the Watts district of Los Angeles led to 30 deaths, and left much of the area in flames. Deaths of the year included Winston Churchill, Adlai Stevenson, Nat "King" Cole and Dr. Albert Schweitzer. But on the

brighter side, Sandy Koufax pitched two shutouts during the World Series, giving the Los Angeles Dodgers a 4-to-3 victory over the Minnesota Twins.

Motion pictures during 1955 included *Rebel Without a Cause* (James Dean), *The Seven Year Itch* (Marilyn Monroe), *Mister Roberts* (Henry Fonda), *Oklahoma* (Shirley Jones and Gordon MacRae), and the Disney cartoon, *Lady and the Tramp*. Academy Awards that year went to *Marty* (Best Picture), Ernest Borgnine (Best Actor, for *Marty*) and Anna Magnani (Best Actress, for The Rose Tattoo).

A decade later we were watching *The Yellow Rolls-Royce* (Rex Harrison, Jeanne Moreau, George C. Scott, Ingrid Bergman, Omar Sharif — what a cast!); *The Sandpiper* (Elizabeth Taylor and Richard Burton); *What's New Pussycat* (Peter Sellers and Peter O'Toole). Academy Awards went to *The Sound of Music* (Best Picture), Lee Marvin (Best Actor, for *Cat Ballou*) and Julie Christie (Best Actress, for *Darling*).

Fiction, during 1955, included McKinley Kantor's *Andersonville*, which went on to win the Pulitzer prize during 1956; *Auntie Mame*, which soon became a major Broadway hit; and Herman Wouk's *Marjorie*

Morningstar. Ten years later, leading the list were James Michener's *The Source*; Arthur Hailey's *Hotel*; and Bel Kaufman's hilarious *Up the Down Staircase*.

It was during this decade — 1955 to 1965 — that television invaded virtually every American home. The fad at the beginning of this period was the quiz show, which ended in scandal in 1959 when it became known that answers were being fed by the sponsors to certain contestants.

And of course, as always, Americans were humming their favorite tunes. Hits during 1955 included "Cry Me a River," popularized by Julie London; "Sixteen Tons," a big hit for "Tennessee Ernie" Ford; and the Academy Award-winning "Love Is a Many Splendored Thing." Ten years later the big ones included "Goldfinger," from the James Bond film of the same name; "I Will Wait for You," written by Michel Legrand and featured in the superb French film, *The Umbrellas of Cherbourg*; and "The Shadow of Your Smile" (from *The Sandpiper*), another Academy Award winner.

And so it went. As they say, "The more things change, the more they stay the same."

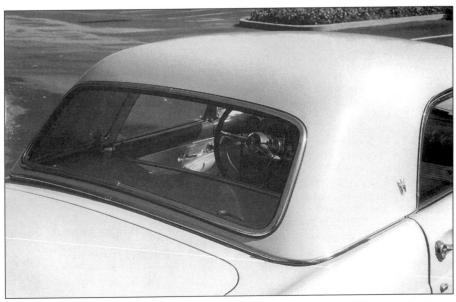

Top left: T-Bird's steering column adjusts. Exhausts/bumper guards follow round taillamp design. *Above and below:* With tops up (or on), rear visibility in either car is adequate. *Bottom:* Thunderbird's dash has more of a pure sports car appearance.

satisfyingly brisk. Walt Woron, noting that the T-Bird "can burn rubber when changing gears (even with a Ford-O-Matic)," figured 11 seconds for the zero-to-60 run, while Tom McCahill — an aggressive driver if ever there was one! — covered the same ground in 9.6 seconds. Either way you look at it, this car is quick.

The seating position is very low, and having survived back surgery last year, I expected problems in that respect. I need not have been concerned, for I was quite comfortable, partly because the telescopic steering column provides a variety of positions, and partly because of the optional four-way power seat. The ride is good, too: firm enough to provide the 'Bird with excellent cornering characteristics, but soft enough to be very comfortable.

Steering is reasonably quick, at three and a half turns, lock-to-lock; and the power assist provides more "road feel" than I've found in either Chrysler or General Motors products of this vintage. And the brakes appear to be very good, an opinion confirmed by Walt Woron, who called them "well above average." As these cars left the factory, they were fitted with tubeless tires, making the Thunderbirds the first American cars to be so equipped.

These first-generation Thunderbirds came with a removable fiberglass hardtop as standard equipment, while a folding canvas top was available at extra cost. (The little "porthole" that one often sees on the "Little Birds" was not available in 1955; it came along in '56.) The trunk isn't as cramped as one might expect, but it is not roomy enough to accommodate the hardtop, which must be left at home when not in use.

Sharp-eyed readers may question the 1951 date on the T-Bird's front license plate. It's legitimate. During the mid-

1950's California issued a small tab each year, in order to update the license. But only one tab was issued, and regulations required that it be displayed on the rear plate.

Other items of interest include the air scoop on the hood. It's for real. A bib on the air cleaner directs air from the scoop to the standard four-barrel carburetor. A block-off plate was available for use during cold weather. The hood opens from the rear, after the manner of certain Hudson models. (At least, one can be sure it won't fly up in the driver's face in the event that the latch fails.)

Standard instruments include a tachometer and a clock, flanking the speedometer, as well as fuel and temperature gauges. "Idiot" lights warn of trouble with the oil pressure and electrical system.

The earliest Thunderbird was — and is — an outstanding little automobile, but it is not without its drawbacks. The dual exhausts, exiting through bumper pods, are an invitation to rust and corrosion. There are no sun visors, a feature that was added in 1956. Nor is the car equipped with vent wings, with the result that its occupants are aware of considerable wind turbulence at speed.

But these are minor faults in an otherwise fine car.

Our Mustang is an early example of the genre. Its serial number indicates, in fact, that it was assembled at the San Jose plant during the first week of July 1964, right after that factory started producing Mustangs.

Although the Mustang falls, like the Thunderbird, in the "sporty personal car" category, the two cars differ sharply in a number of respects. For one thing, there's the matter of cost. Adjusted for inflation, the $330 difference between them grows to about $950 — more than a third of the Mustang's base price. Then there's the weight: Despite the fact that the Mustang has double the passenger capacity of the 'Bird, it is the lighter of the two by well over 300 pounds, thanks in part to its use of unitized construction. And although the difference in displacement isn't all that great, the 'Bird's Y-block V-8 is considerably heavier than the more modern Mustang engine. We'll point out other distinctions as we go along.

Our featured Mustang is on the road virtually every weekend, driven either by its owner, Joe Cristiano, or by one or another of Joe's six kids. It was one of Joe's sons, in fact, who purchased the car in 1986. Although it had logged only 67,000 miles at that time, it obviously had not led an easy life, and it needed a lot of help. The restoration, which be-

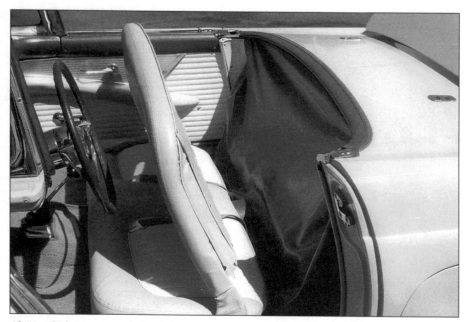

Above: Soft top stows behind Thunderbird's thinly padded seats. **Below:** With just six more inches in total length compared to the 'Bird, Mustang can accommodate four people inside.

came a father-and-son project (with some outside help), took about a year to complete.

The engine turned out to be in good shape, but the Cristianos found it necessary to overhaul the Cruise-O-Matic transmission, rear end, brakes and exhaust system. New wiring was also required, for each time the turn signals were used, the horn would blow. A new interior kit was installed, but paint and top remain untouched. Both will probably have been renewed by the time this article is in print.

Like the Thunderbird, the Mustang — which by now has covered some 113,000 miles — is a lively car; though the 'Bird is the faster of the two by a rather substantial margin. This seat-of-the-pants assessment is clearly borne out by road test results, as compiled by Tom McCahill. In large measure this reflects the difference in gearing between the stick-and-overdrive T-Bird and the automatic Mustang. But partly it has to do with horsepower and torque in both of which the Y-block engine of the 'Bird enjoys a significant advantage. Even so, we're told that the Mustang will cruise without strain at 85 miles per

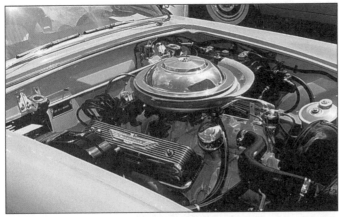

Above: With lots of chrome plating, T-Bird engine is the more eye-catching of the two. **Below:** *Thunderbird's door panels are flashier, too.*
Bottom: *But at the rear they both look sufficiently sporty.*

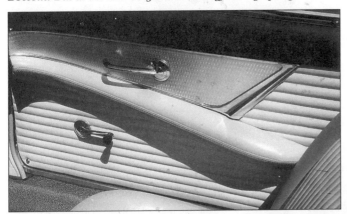

SIA comparisonReport

hour, if the highway patrol isn't looking.

As for what it's like to drive the Mustang, even Tom McCahill regarded it as "a beautifully handling car. The steering and control have to be rated A for a general-travel car." Once again, the power steering is a nice unit, preserving in considerable measure the feel of the road. The car corners well, though possibly not quite as flat as the Thunderbird. The Cruise-O-Matic transmission, controlled by a console-mounted T-handle, shifts crisply, yet smoothly through the gears. The brakes do their job well, though they don't feel quite as powerful as those of the T-Bird. That figures, since the 'Bird's binders have larger drums and about one-third more effective area.

The driver sits low in this car, just as

he does in the Thunderbird. Front leg room is quite adequate, though quarters are a little tight in the rear. Head room is surprisingly generous. The ride is good, by light car standards, though it does not fully measure up to the Thunderbird in that respect.

Typically, in preparing these comparisonReports, we try to assess which car has the advantage over the other. That's not really a feasible assignment in this case, partly because of the ten-year age difference between the two machines, and partly because, despite having a number of characteristics in common, they are quite different in concept. The Mustang was clearly built to a price, and a bargain it was. The Thunderbird, on the other hand, almost represents a cost-is-no-object endeavor. It is a premium-quality product throughout.

As to this writer's personal preference, once again, that's hard to say. Hands

down, I would like the Thunderbird better, provided I did not have need for a back seat. On the other hand, when it comes to dollar value, it's the Mustang's game all the way. Each car, it seems to me, is outstanding in its own way. Each was ahead of its time. Each is fun to drive, and each of them has certainly proven to be an outstanding investment on the part of its original owner. ❏

Acknowledgments and Bibliography
Automotive Industries, *March 15, 1955;* Automotive Industries, *March 15, 1965;* Huntington, Roger, *"Performance Rating Factors for All 1955 Cars,"* Motor Life, *May 1955;* Lewis, David L., Mike McCarville and Lorin Sorensen, Ford: 1903-1984; McCahill, Tom, *"Ford's All-New Mustang,"* Mechanix Illustrated, *July, 1964;* McCahill, Tom, *"The Ford Thunderbird,"* Mechanix Illustrated, *January 1955;* Witzenburg, Gary L., Mustang: The Complete History of America's Pioneer Ponycar; *Woron, Walt, "Ford Thunderbird,"* Motor Trend, *December 1954;* "Ford Thunderbird," Road and Track, *October 1954;* "Ford's Young One," Time, *April 17, 1964;* "The Mustang — A New Breed Out of Detroit," Newsweek, *April 20, 1964;* 1964 Auto Bluebook.
Our thanks to Gil Baumgartner, Suisun, California; Ralph Dunwoodie, Sun Valley, Nevada; Ben Gostanian, Fresno, California. Special thanks to Joe Cristiano, Pleasanton, California; Brent Hokanson, Fairfield, California.

1965 Falcon vs. 1965 Mustang

by Alex Meredith
photos by Bud Juneau

IT would be difficult to imagine two more dissimilar personalities than Robert Strange McNamara and Lido Anthony Iacocca. Yet each of them in turn was responsible for one of the Ford Motor Company's major success stories.

McNamara, a former Harvard professor, was—as Robert Lacey has noted—"a puritan." He looked the part, too, with his hair parted in the middle, his low-key demeanor, his rimless "granny" glasses and conservatively tailored suits. And although he spent 15 years in Ford's employ, rising ultimately to the presidency of the organization, there was no gasoline flowing in his veins. McNamara obviously viewed the automobile as nothing more than transportation.

The car for which Professor McNamara is best remembered reflects his personality. Conventionally styled, no frills, designed for easy maintenance, it represented a return to the basics, a sort of latter-day Model A. It was, of course, the 1960 Falcon. And in its time the Falcon was the best-selling new car the company had ever introduced.

Iacocca, on the other hand, could be thought of as McNamara's opposite number. Completely opposite! The son of proud, fiercely independent Italian immigrant parents, he proudly boasts that he "came up the hard way." Flamboyant, profane, enthusiastic by nature, and a born salesman, he has carried on a lifelong love affair with the automobile. To Iacocca the car is—or at any rate ought to be—the extension of its owner's personality.

So it comes as no surprise that it was Iacocca who was responsible for transforming McNamara's staid Falcon into the sporty, high-styled, youth-oriented Mustang. Once again, just as the Falcon had done, the new model reflected the personality of its mentor. And once again, the new car broke all previous first-year sales records—including that of the Falcon.

The Falcon made its debut on October 8, 1959, six days after the introduction of Chevrolet's rear-engined Corvair. Both were designed, as was Chrysler's Valiant, to capitalize on the rapidly growing economy-car market. And from a sales standpoint it was simply no contest. Production for that initial model year—1960—came to 435,676 Falcons, 250,007 Corvairs and 194,292 Valiants. By avoiding the mechanical sophistication of the Corvair and the styling extremes of the Valiant. McNamara—vice president, at the time, for all of Ford's car and truck divisions—had produced a winner.

It was strictly a plain-Jane automobile. Power came from an 85-horsepower, 144-cubic-inch, overhead-valve

six. Body styles, that first year, were confined to two- and four-door sedans and two- and four-door station wagons. The option list was short. The two-speed Ford-O-Matic transmission ($159) was quite popular, despite the severe penalty it exacted from the Falcon's already marginal performance. There was a dress-up trim package ($66), heater/defroster ($68), and a radio ($54). But no power steering or brakes, and no air-conditioner, which would have placed an intolerable burden on the diminutive engine.

By 1961 a much more robust 170-c.i.d. engine was a $37 option, and a dolled-up two-door model featuring bucket seats and console was added to

the line as the "Futura."

Meanwhile, on November 2, 1959, Lido "Lee" Iacocca had become vice president of the Ford Division, and on January 3, 1961, Robert McNamara had left Dearborn to become Secretary of Defense in President John F. Kennedy's cabinet.

Ford was about to experience some changes.

Iacocca moved quickly to add a little pizzazz to the Falcon image. A "Squire" station wagon, complete with ersatz wood trim, was added to the 1962 line, and at mid-season the Futura was given a squared-off, Thunderbird-inspired roofline. It wasn't until 1963, however, that the Falcon felt the full impact of Lee

Iacocca's fine Italian hand. Changes were numerous that year, and highly visible:

• The Futura became an upscale Falcon series, consisting of two- and four-door sedans (the former supplied with either bench or bucket seats), and Falcon's first convertibles — three of them, including the sporty Sprint version, a mid-season offering. Also new at mid-year was a pair of high-styled, semi-fastback hardtop coupes. No longer did the Falcon wear Professor McNamara's granny glasses.

• All Falcon sedans adopted the Thunderbird-inspired roofline, first featured on the 1962½ Futura.

• V-8 power became available in the form of Ford's 260-c.i.d. small block engine, providing outstanding performance at surprisingly little sacrifice in economy.

• A four-speed transmission was offered at extra cost.

Changes for 1964 were more modest, yet even more visible. The Falcon was re-skinned below the belt line, giving it a series of horizontal creases which strengthened the sheet metal while tending to make the car appear longer and lower. The 200-c.i.d., 120-horsepower Fairlane six became a Falcon option that year, supplying a welcome dose of vitamins at modest additional cost.

Then at mid-year the Mustang came galloping into view, cannibalizing Falcon sales — particularly those of the sporty hardtop and convertible body styles. At the same time, the mid-sized

Taillamp treatment couldn't be more different. Falcon uses a variation on traditional Ford round lamp design while Mustang carries distinctive tri-section rectangles.

Fairlane, first introduced in 1962, had lured away substantial numbers of sedan and station wagon buyers.

If the original Falcon represented an extension of Robert McNamara's bland personality, surely the flashy little Mustang reflected the extroverted Iacocca. Not that he actually designed the car, but reportedly the concept was his, and certainly it was he who pushed the proposal.

The inspiration, however, had come from Chevrolet. The rear-engined Corvair had been anything but a sales sensation in its original guise, that of an economy vehicle. But by 1962 sales of the sporty Monza variant were brisk, accounting for 71.5 percent of the Corvair's total volume. As Iacocca has noted in his autobiography, "We at Ford had nothing to offer to the people who were considering a Monza, but it was clear to us that they represented a growing market."

Meanwhile, Falcon buyers had been opting, in surprising numbers, for larger engines, automatic transmissions and trim items such as white sidewall tires. Clearly there was a market for a sporty, upscale compact car.

The demographics supported this conclusion. The postwar "baby boomers" — hordes of them — were about to enter the automobile market. The number of two-car families was growing fast, and the second car was typically smaller and sportier than the first. Women buyers, their numbers increasing rapidly, tended to prefer smaller, more maneuverable cars — as well as stylish ones. "Whereas the Edsel had been a car in search of a market it never found," Lee

1965 Comparison Table: Compact Four-Door Sedans

	Ford Falcon	Chevy II	Chevy Corvair	Rambler American	Plymouth Valiant
Price, base 4-door sedan	$2,082	$2,115	$2,142	$2,036	$2,075
HP/c.i.d. std. 6-cyl. engine	105/170	120/194	95/164	90/195.6	101/170
HP/c.i.d., opt. 6-cyl. engine	120/200	140/230	110/164	155/232	145/225
HP/c.i.d., base V-8 engine	200/289	195/283	N/a	N/a	180/273
Front springing	Coils	Coils	Coils	Coils	Torsion Bars
Braking area (sq. in.)	114.3	168.9	168.9	139.5	153.5
Tire size (standard)	6.00/13	6.50/13	6.50/13	6.45/14	6.50/13
Wheelbase	109.5 inches	110 inches	108 inches	106 inches	106 inches
Overall length	181.6 inches	182.9 inches	183.3 inches	177.3 inches	188.2 inches
Overall height	54.5 inches	55.0 inches	51.2 inches	54.5 inches	53.5 inches
Overall width	71.6 inches	69.9 inches	69.7 inches	70.9 inches	70.1 inches
Weight (pounds)	2,410	2,670	2,405	2,518	2,590
Final drive ratio (std. trans.)	3.20:1	3.08:1	3.27:1	3.08:1	3.23:1
Optional automatic transmission	3-speed	2-speed	2-speed	3-speed	3-speed
Production (model year)	185,927	118,115	235,500*	112,883	153,576

* 77 percent of Corvair production consisted of Monza and Corsa models.

Iacocca recalls, "here was a market in search of a car.... We were in a position... to tailor a new product for a hungry new market."

It was evident that if a new car was to be successfully marketed, the price would have to be reasonable, which meant that both development and production costs would have to be held to a minimum. Ford had taken a monumental bath with the Edsel, and heavy retooling expenses would be incurred in connection with the new full-sized Ford, planned for 1965. So venture capital was in short supply. Some of the company's senior executives viewed the "sporty car" proposal with skepticism.

But Iacocca pushed ahead. By using components borrowed from the Falcon, he reasoned, the investment could be held to something like $75 million — less than a quarter of what an entirely new car would cost. Still, there were doubters. Iacocca recalls that one of Ford's product planners commented that "making a sporty car out of a Falcon was like putting falsies on grandma."

The styling department came up with no fewer than 18 clay models, none of which seemed to be quite right. The pressure was on; Iacocca's goal was to have the new car ready for display at the opening of the New York World's Fair, in April 1964 — just 21 months away. To speed the process, styling director Gene Bordinat staged a contest among the Ford, Lincoln-Mercury and corporate styling studios, charging each of them to come up with at least one clay model, and have it ready in just 20 days. Impossible! Or so it must have seemed, but when the deadline arrived there were seven models to choose from.

The winning proposal — tentatively called the Cougar — was submitted by Dave Ash, assistant to Ford studio chief Joe Oros. With its long hood/short deck configuration and its smart, crisp lines, it "looked like it was moving," Iacocca recalls, "although it was just sitting there on the studio floor."

The critical challenge was that of selling the "Cougar" to Henry Ford II. Fortunately, he was enthusiastic, although he mandated (wisely, in our view) that an extra inch be added to the rear seat leg room. That there were risks involved in the project, Ford fully understood, but to Iacocca he confided, "if you want to be in this business and not lose your mind, you've got to be a little bold!"

For reasons that are not altogether clear, the Cougar name was dropped in favor of "Mustang," which had been the title of one of the unsuccessful styling proposals. Curiously, the original reference was to the famed World War II fighter plane, rather than the animal, but the wild horse quickly became the new car's mascot.

There's not a lot of family resemblance in the grille designs, either. Falcon is modeled after big Fords while Mustang is unlike anything else from Dearborn.

Table of Prices, Weights and Production

1965 Falcon

	Price	Weight	Production
Falcon Series			
Sedan, 4-door	$2,038	2,410	30,186
Sedan, 2-door	$1,977	2,370	35,858
Futura Series			
Sedan, 4-door	$2,146	2,410	33,985
Sedan, 2-door	$2,099	2,375	11,670
Hardtop Coupe	$2,179	2,395	24,451
Hardtop Coupe (bucket seats)	$2,226	2,380	1,303
Convertible	$2,428	2,675	6,191
Convertible (bucket seats)	$2,481	2,660	124
"Sprint" Hardtop	$2,425	2,813	2,806
"Sprint" Convertible	$2,660	2,695	300
Station Wagon Series			
Falcon Wagon, 4-door	$2,317	2,680	14,911
Falcon Wagon, 2-door	$2,284	2,640	4,891
Futura Wagon	$2,453	2,670	12,548
Squire Wagon	$2,608	2,695	6,703
TOTAL			185,927

1965 Mustang

	Price	Weight	Production*
Hardtop Coupe	$2,372	2,405	409,260
Fastback Coupe	$2,589	2,515	77,079
Convertible	$2,614	2,650	73,112
TOTAL			559,451

* Production figures do not include Mustangs built prior to October 1, 1964 (sometimes known as the "1964½" models)

All prices are f.o.b. factory, with standard equipment, federal excise tax and preparation charges included.

Both Falcon and Mustang corner competently and without excessive lean while delivering a comfortable ride over most surfaces.

SIA comparisonReport

The use of Falcon components enabled Ford to keep the Mustang's base price as low as $2,368 for the six-cylinder hardtop. V-8 power cost another $108, and a wide range of options was available. Luxury touches included the Cruise-O-Matic transmission ($179.80 with the "six," $189.60 with the V-8), power steering ($86.30), power brakes ($43.20) and air conditioner ($283.20). Or the performance buff could tailor the Mustang to his own preferences by adding the 271-horsepower V-8 ($442.60), four-speed manual transmission ($75.80 with V-8 power), special handling package ($31.30), limited-slip differential ($42.50) and front disc brakes ($58). Thus the Mustang became — depending upon the option list — a car of many personalities.

Although it made the scene on schedule, in April 1964, the original Mustang was billed as a 1965 model. This was

Comparative Specifications
1965 Falcon and Mustang Sixes

	Falcon	Mustang
Price (f.o.b. factory with standard equipment)	$2,481	$2,614
Options on feature cars	200-c.i.d. engine, Cruise-O-Matic transmission, radio, wire wheel covers, rocker panel molding, backup lamps, luggage compartment light, interior light group, 14-inch wheels, 2-speed wiper with windshield washer	Radio, white sidewall tires
Engines (identical in both cars)	In-line, 6-cylinder	Same
Bore x stroke	3 11/16" x 3⅛"	3 11/16" x 3⅛"
Displacement	200.2 cu. in.	200.2 cu. in.
Compression ratio	9.20:1	9.20:1
Max. bhp @ rpm	120 @ 4,400	120 @ 4,400
Max. torque @ rpm	190 @ 2,400	190 @ 2,400
Taxable horsepower	32.5	32.5
Valve configuration	Ohv	Ohv
Valve lifters	Hydraulic	Hydraulic
Main bearings	Seven	Seven
Induction system	1-bbl carburetor, mechanical pump	1-bbl carburetor, mechanical pump
Lubrication system	Pressure	Pressure
Exhaust system	Single	Single
Electrical system	12-volt	12-volt
Clutch	N/a	Single dry plate
Diameter		8½"
Actuation		Mechanical, foot pedal
Transmission	Cruise-O-Matic 3-speed automatic	3-speed manual, floor lever
Ratios	2.46/1.46/1.00 (2.20 reverse)	2.76/1.69/1.00 (3.74 reverse)
Max ratio at stall (torque conv)	2.14	N/a
Differential	Hypoid	Hypoid
Ratio	2.83:1	3.20:1
Drive axles	Semi-floating	Semi-floating
Steering	Manual	Manual
Turns, lock to lock	4¾	5
Ratios	19.9 gear, 27.0 overall	19.9 gear, 27.0 overall
Turning circle	38' 10" (curb/curb)	38' 11" (curb/curb)
Brakes (identical, both cars)	4-wheel hydraulic drum type	4-wheel hydraulic drum type
Drum diameter	9 inches	9 inches
Effective area	114.3 sq. in.	114.3 sq. in.
Chassis and body	All-steel unitized	All-steel unitized
Body style	Convertible coupe	Convertible coupe
Front suspension	Ball joint type w/coil springs pivot-mounted on upper arms. Link stabilizer	Ball joint type w/coil springs mounted on upper arms. Link-type stabilizer
Rear suspension	Conventional, semi-elliptic springs	Conventional, semi-elliptic springs
Tires (factory equipment)	6.45/14	6.50/13
Tires (present)	P195/75-14	P185/80-B13
Wheels	Pressed steel, drop-center rims	Pressed steel, drop-center rims
Crankcase capacity	3½ quarts (less filter)	3½ quarts (less filter)
Transmission capacity	15 pints	2½ pints
Cooling system (w/heater)	19 pints	19 pints
Fuel tank	14 gallons	16 gallons
Wheelbase	109.5 inches	108.0 inches
Overall length	181.6 inches	181.6 inches
Overall width	71.6 inches	68.2 inches
Overall height	53.8 inches	51.1 inches
Track, front/rear	55.0"/56.0"	55.4"/56.0"
Trunk volume (cu. ft.)	9.1	7.7
Ground clearance (min.)	5.6 inches	5.2 inches
Shipping weight	2,675 pounds	2,650 pounds
Horsepower/c.i.d.	.599	.599
Pounds/horsepower	22.3	22.1
Pounds/c.i.d.	13.4	13.2
Pounds/sq. in. (brakes)	23.4	23.2

largely a fiction, however, for on October 1, 1964, a revised version appeared. Styling was unchanged, but the second series 1965s — some call them the "true" '65s — were more powerful: The 200 and 289-c.i.d. engines replaced the 170 and 260, respectively, as the standard powerplants. And a new fastback was added to the original hardtop and convertible configurations. Prices, remarkably enough, were unchanged.

In the meanwhile the Falcon had not been standing still. Visually there was little difference in the 1965 model, although a new grille was adopted. But the 144-cubic-inch engine was dropped, the 289-c.i.d. V-8 replaced the 260, and the three-speed Cruise-O-Matic transmission was substituted for the less efficient Ford-O-Matic. Most of the options offered on the Mustang were also available for the Falcon. But buyers were quick to note that by the time a Falcon convertible was outfitted with bucket seats and the 200-c.i.d. engine — both standard issue on the second series 1965 Mustang — the

Above and below: The two cars share door hardware, but Mustang panels have sportier appearance than Falcon's. Right: Power top was an option on Mustangs, standard on Falcon.

SIA comparisonReport

1965: Transition Time
by Dave Brown

When we remind ourselves of what made American culture of the 1960s unique, the features we remember best were either unfolding or just achieving their full form in 1965.

Lyndon Johnson had turned a presidency acquired through the assassination of John Kennedy into a mandate in the 1964 election. Early in the year his administration launched the "Great Society," a wide ranging social agenda built upon but eclipsing the previous generation's "New Deal." The Civil Rights movement reached a climax with Martin Luther King's march on Selma, Alabama, that spring. In August, rioting in the Watts district of Los Angeles brought the black urban ghetto into the consciousness of middle America.

By means of the now ubiquitous television set, scenes of an escalating war effort in Southeast Asia became familiar to us all. We winced in November when a massive power outage in the Northeast underscored our dependence on technology, then cheered in December when the same scientific expertise enabled astronauts

Frank Borman and James Lovell, Jr. to orbit the earth 206 times.

Eldest members of the "baby boom" generation, born following World War II, were graduating from high school in 1965 and commencing to enter adulthood. If only because of the sheer numbers they could muster, their agenda had an impact on their elders. Long hair, sandals and marijuana use commenced to be seen; a "generation gap" had begun. Rock and roll music, with us now for a decade, had proven its staying power. Now, however, its light, romantic lyrics were supplemented with a brand of social commentary known as the "protest" song.

Moviegoers in 1965 watched Peter Sellers and Peter O'Toole in *What's New Pussycat*, along with *Cat Ballou*, starring Lee Marvin. The reading list included James Michener's *The Source* and Eric Berne's *Games People Play*.

For many of us, the sixties were good times. Still, by 1965 we had lost the unbridled and perhaps excessive optimism of the fifties.

Somehow the world didn't feel quite as comfortable as it once had been.

price differential was only $78. Not surprisingly, the soft-top Mustang outsold its Falcon counterpart by a margin of eleven to one.

As matters developed, 1965 was the last year for the Falcon's original 109½-inch wheelbase, as well as the final appearance of the hardtop and convertible body styles. For 1966 the Falcon would become, in effect, a truncated (and rather clumsily proportioned) version of the Fairlane. Larger, heavier (by 150 pounds) and somewhat more expensive than the 1965 model, it had lost whatever sporting pretensions the Falcon had acquired along the way, and it had strayed far from the original Falcon concept. Not until the coming of the Maverick, in mid-1969, would Ford again market a McNamara-style, back-to-basics compact car.

Driving Impressions

Until recently very little attention was paid to the six-cylinder Mustangs, although more than a third of the 1965 models were powered by that engine. And even less attention has been given by collectors to the Falcon, a situation which appears to be changing now. So in order to help fill the gap, *SIA* has undertaken to compare the Falcon six and its more glamorous counterpart.

(We almost said "offspring." But how can a bird beget a horse?)

Both of our comparisonReport cars are powered by the 200-c.i.d., 120-horsepower engine, standard issue for the Mustang, optional at extra cost in the Falcon. This seven-bearing, overhead-

*Left: Neither car has overwhelming trunk space as top storage area chews up square footage. **Above and below:** Out back, both cars exhibit restrained design with Mustang the plainer of the two.*

valve "six" is a vastly better unit than the original Falcon engine, introduced in 1960. Not only was the 144-c.i.d., four-bearing version badly underpowered, but its lubrication system tended to starve the valve train, creating a most unpleasant clatter. The 200-cubic-inch job, on the other hand, is both durable and quiet, as well as substantially more powerful. Good enough, in fact, to have served to power Ford Fairmont and Mercury Zephyr models into the 1980s.

Standard equipment for both Falcon and Mustang was a three-speed manual transmission, with the three-speed Cruise-O-Matic available at extra cost. Here we were able to observe the contrast, for our Mustang is fitted with the stick shift while the Falcon has the automatic. The latter, a very smooth performer, carries with it a taller axle ratio: 2.83:1 in lieu of 3.20:1. Neither car is equipped with the optional power-assisted steering or brakes. Nor, in our view, is the power equipment really needed for these light and nicely balanced cars.

Our comparisonReport Falcon was in pretty sad shape when it was acquired by its present owner, Eddie Call, of Stockton, California. First sold in Philadelphia, it had been driven to Los Angeles in the mid-1970s by its second owner. A third buyer started out in the early 1980s on a trip to the Pacific Northwest, but he got only as far as Stockton, about halfway up California's great Central Valley, before the car died. Having no money for repairs, he sold the little ragtop, and at that point Eddie Call acquired it.

Surprisingly, since it had been an East Coast car for many years, there was no rust in evidence. But there was extensive body damage. The right side had

been bashed in, virtually all the brightwork needed replacement, and most of the sheet metal had been massaged. The engine had been rebuilt fairly recently, but the transmission needed help and work was needed on the front end.

Eddie haunted the wrecking yards and the swap meets, and answered any number of ads. Doors, front fenders, bumpers, vent wings, taillamps, headlamp bezels, fuel tank and other components were replaced with good used parts. A new old stock grille was located, along with new side trim. Reproduction carpets and trunk mat were installed.

And then the car was sent to the body shop at San Joaquin Delta Community College, where the students — under the watchful eye of instructor George Nishimoto — undertook to straighten the body panels and repaint the car in its original Honey Gold color. Their thoroughly professional work speaks well

for both the students and their instructor.

The Mustang, too, had sustained body damage to the right side, necessitating replacement of the right door and the right rear clip. In general, however, its body was in better shape than that of the Falcon when it was acquired by its present owner, Dick Albrecht, another Stockton resident.

Assembled at Ford's Milpitas plant, this car was first sold in nearby San Jose. Exactly when it passed to the hands of its second owner, we have been unable to learn, but in any event this lady was a marine biologist who was overseas much of the time. Consequently the Mustang has logged only 78,000 miles to date — scarcely more than half the total racked up by Eddie Call's Falcon.

Even so, a great deal of effort was required in order to bring the Mustang to its present condition. The engine was

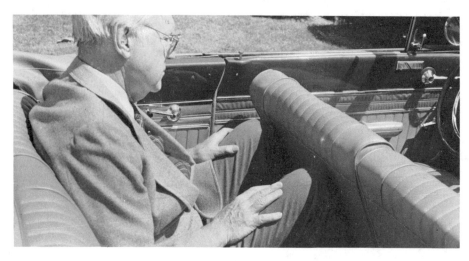

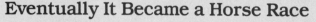

SIA comparisonReport

Eventually It Became a Horse Race

Back in 1965 the Mustang's only competitors in the "sporty personal car" field were the Chevy Monza and Corsa, and the Plymouth Barracuda. The former were upscale, bucket-seated versions of the Corvair, while the latter was a fastback derivative of the Valiant hardtop featuring an enormous, 2,074-square-inch backlight.

But by 1965 there was no shortage of competitors for the Falcon. Chevrolet offered both the Corvair, a highly unusual machine, at least by American standards, and the totally conventional Chevy II. Chrysler Corporation had the Plymouth Valiant and its slightly stretched companion, the Dodge Dart. From American Motors came the Rambler American, the little car that must be credited with starting it all. And Ford's own Lincoln-Mercury Division supplied the Comet, a longer-wheelbase version of the Falcon.

Among this group of compact cars, some interesting comparisons can be drawn.

- The Rambler offered the lowest standard horsepower and the only L-head engine in the group, but its optional ohv powerplant was the most powerful six in the field.
- Falcon supplied the biggest standard V-8 — but the smallest brakes.

- Chevrolet's Corvair was the lightest car in the group, while the Chevy II was the heaviest.
- Only the Corvair offered an air-cooled rear engine and independent rear suspension.
- Torsion bar front suspension was exclusive to the Valiant and its near-twin, the Dart.

Thus the economy-minded 1965 motorist could choose among a wide field of reasonably priced, highly competent small cars, cars which laid the groundwork for the sporty derivatives that would follow in later years. For in time, "pony cars" (the term itself serves to credit Ford with having originated the genre) would be derived from each of these compacts, excepting only the Corvair. Arriving on the scene for 1967 was the Chevrolet Camaro, offspring of the Chevy II, as well as Mercury's handsome Cougar. That same year there was a second-generation Barracuda — this one much more sharply differentiated than before, at least in terms of styling, from the Valiant. American Motors joined the horse race in 1968 with the Javelin (see SIA #94), with Dodge belatedly fielding the Challenger in 1970.

All of which was more than even Lee Iacocca could have predicted.

rebuilt; new wheel bearings and axle seals were installed; the brakes were overhauled; top, upholstery and carpeting were all replaced; and the car was repainted in Phoenician Yellow, its original hue. Much of the work was done by Dick Albrecht himself, with finishing touches applied by Robert Garza, of Manteca, California.

Both cars, we found, corner without excessive lean, though their suspension is tuned more for comfort than for performance. Steering, again in both instances, is pleasantly light but somewhat slow. Acceleration, we'd say, is adequate in the Cruise-O-Matic equipped Falcon, and distinctly better (though by no means neck-snapping) in the stick-shift Mustang.

The Mustang's clutch is stiff, and its action is deceptive. Pushed two-thirds of the way to the floor, it feels as though it has released. But it hasn't; a further shove is required before the gear change can safely be made. We suspect that some adjustment may be needed here. The shift linkage is a little balky. Nothing has been done to the transmission in this car, and we think it may need some help.

Braking area in these machines is a little skimpy, compared to the competition, but although fairly heavy pedal pressure is required, we were pleasantly surprised at how well the binders work. *Motor Trend*, road-testing a 1963 Falcon with brakes identical to those of both of our comparisonReport cars, noted: "We used the brakes hard...but

Left: One reason why the Mustang could sell for so little. The engine came straight from Falcon. **Above and below:** Although both cars offered sixes and V-8s, Mustang quickly emerged as the car with sports car image and performance.

didn't notice any excessive fade or pedal pressure build-up. During the actual brake tests, they performed exceptionally well."

Both of these convertibles are snug and rattle-free, but the Falcon seems to be better insulated than the Mustang (an impression reinforced, no doubt, by its taller gears). Certainly we were less aware of road noise in the Falcon. In all honesty the Falcon seems to be finished off better than the Mustang, and — at least in one respect — better equipped. That is, the power top, standard equipment on Falcon convertibles, cost extra on the Mustang. (Our test car didn't have it, but the one-man manual top is easy to operate.)

Both cars offer adequate front leg room. We happen to be partial to bucket seats, which the Mustang has but the Falcon does not. Even so, the Falcon seats seemed to us to have the edge in terms of comfort.

But it's in the back seat where the contrast is most apparent. The Falcon is reasonably comfortable. Even a six-footer can find room for his knees, with the front seat pushed all the way back. Not so the Mustang! It's cramped. Even with the extra inch of space mandated by Henry Ford II that rear compartment could keep a lot of chiropractors in business. Similarly, the luggage space provided by the Mustang is quite limited.

The bottom line in any comparison-Report is which to choose, if the calendar were turned back to the time when these cars were new. If we had been asked that question before we undertook this comparison, our instinctive response would have been "The Mustang!" Now, however, we're not so sure.

Obviously, the Mustang has the clear

advantage in styling. This, in our view, is one of the great designs of the post-war era. Equally obviously, it's miles ahead as an investment. A nice Mustang convertible must be worth at least twice as much as the equivalent Falcon, though a few years ago the difference would have been even greater.

But if the cars are regarded as transportation, which after all was their intended purpose in the first place, a different answer emerges. For the Falcon is roomier, quieter, more comfortable, better equipped and seemingly better finished than the Mustang. □

Acknowledgements and Bibliography
Automotive Industries, *March 15, 1965; Ford Motor Company factory literature; John Gunnell, editor,* Encyclopedia of American Cars, 1946-1975; *Lee Iacocca (with William Novak),* Iacocca; *Steve Kelly, "Mustangs,"* Motor Trend, *June 1966; Robert Lacey,* Ford: The Men and the Machine; *Richard M. Langworth,* Encyclopedia of American Cars, 1940-1970; *David L. Lewis, Mike McCarville, and Lorin Sorensen,* Ford, 1903 to 1984; *Jim Wright, "Falcon,"* Motor Trend, *December 1962; "Ford's Young One,"* Time, *April 17, 1964; "Mustang — A New Breed Out of Detroit,"* Newsweek, *April 20, 1964; "Robert Strange McNamara,"* Time, *November 12, 1960.*
Our thanks to Ray Borges, Collections Manager, William F. Harrah Automobile Foundation, Reno, Nevada; Bob Carl, Stockton, California; Dave Brown, Durham, California. Special thanks to Dick Albrecht, Stockton, California; Eddie Call, Stockton, California.

1965 MUSTANG GT 2+2

Driving Impressions

by John F. Katz
photos by Vince Wright

OUR featured Mustang is a 2+2 GT with the Interior Decor Group, built on June 4, 1965, and purchased on June 22 by Harry Harne, Jr., of Frederick, Maryland. Harry had stopped by Reed Motor Co. to check the status of a Mustang he had ordered; he saw our driveReport car backing off the transporter, and drove it home instead.

Harry owned the car until 1970. It then passed through at least one other owner, and one more used car lot, before Terry Sherman of Mt. Airy, Maryland, bought it to build into a drag racer. Sherman cut out the console for a com-

petition shifter, installed a nine-inch, 3.89:1 Traction-Loc rear from a Boss 302, and began converting the outside

of the car to look like a '66 Shelby. He raced it for a while, then stored it, sold it, bought it back, and sold it again. Current owner Nelson Grossnickle bought it in 1988 and brought it all back to stock, interviewing previous owners to authenticate the correct options. He knows for certain that his Mustang left the factory with the GT package, four-speed transmission, console, AM radio, and pony interior. However, he has added a few accessories that probably weren't on the car originally: a Rally Pac clock and tachometer, styled steel wheels, and engine dress-up kit. Ford promoted all three of these items for aftermarket installation, anyway. Nelson's Mustang won its first na-

New Pony in Dearborn's Stable

tional award at a Mustang Club of America show in Lynchburg, Virginia, in 1992; it collected Junior and Senior awards from AACA the following year.

The front bucket seats provide reasonable comfort, with surprisingly good lumbar support, but the steering wheel looms a little close as I reach for the clutch. The shifter, on the other hand, sits too far away—not an uncomfort-

able reach, but not a natural position, either. To compensate for its placement, the lever crooks radically rearward, so that the tiny knob nearly collides with the console in Reverse, Second, or Fourth. Accessory controls all look alike and all require some reaching—in short, average ergonomics for 1965!

The radical roofline blocks vision to the right rear, but not so badly as in some pony/muscle cars that came later. At least there's plenty of room (for two), and you can keep track of both front

fenders thanks to the ridges on top of them.

Powering Nelson's Mustang is the 225-horse 289, driving through the wide-ratio four-speed. This wasn't a popular combination for road tests, as journalists naturally favored the ulti-

mate-output 271-horse unit. But Ford actually sold only 7,273 Hi-Po Mustangs through the extended '65 model year. Figure that half of those went out the door before the GT package even appeared, and we can safely guess that three out of four GT's were powered by

1965 Mustang

Above: Lower body stripes and badges are part of GT package. Below left: Styled steel wheels are original factory option on driveReport car. Right: Stock Mustang taillamps were retained.

The Inevitable Comparison, Part I

Although it debuted a full two weeks ahead of the Mustang—on April 1, 1964—the Plymouth Barracuda achieved neither the celebrity nor the success of its competitor from Dearborn. That the fastback Barracuda shared some of its glass and sheet metal with its parent Valiant couldn't have helped. Still, the appearance of the Mustang Fastback in the fall of '64 made comparisons between the two sporty compacts all the more inevitable.

Around the same time, Chevrolet executives were just beginning to realize that their extensively redesigned '65 Corvair wasn't the answer to the Mustang, either. But the Corvair, too, had its fans.

Motor Trend tested the biggest-engined editions of all three cars for its January '65 issue. And while the editors shied away from direct comparisons, we might infer something from their comments on the individual cars. "Ford's high-performance Mustang won't be everyone's cup of tea," admitted Technical Editor Bob McVay. "But it should give the all-out performance enthusiast just what he's looking for at a price he can afford." With only 235 bhp, the Barracuda clearly couldn't match the Mustang in straight-line performance, but instead earned praise for its people and luggage-carrying versatility, as well as its "Rallye" suspension which greatly enhanced handling with little compromise in ride. *Motor Trend* seemed to see the Corvair Corsa as more of an import fighter, an "answer to American demands for a low-priced European-looking performance/economy car—but with a touch of luxury and

more seating capacity and luggage space than you normally find in imported cars."

Car and Driver hadn't been nearly so reticent when it sampled the same three cars in October '64. "After testing the Corvair, the Mustang fastback, and the Barracuda," wrote Editor David E. Davis, Jr. (in a sidebar titled "Making the inevitable comparison"), "we would be craven cowards indeed if we didn't try to draw some comparative conclusions."

Davis rated the Mustang "very fast and very exciting to drive. Unfortunately, part of this excitement stems from Ford's antique Hotchkiss-drive rear suspension... which allows the back end to slide at a furious pace." The Hi-Po Mustang was less GT, Davis concluded, and more Super Stock—the quickest of the three cars in a straight-line contest. The Formula S Barracuda, on the other hand, "handles the way a man who's had some time in European GT cars would like it to handle," proving itself a far better road car than Dearborn's pony.

But neither horse nor fish, Davis avowed, could equal the sweet charms of the Corvair. "It has a styling treatment that is one full cycle ahead of its competition.... The regular Corvair handles beautifully and needs no heavy-duty suspension. The car's only flaw is the limited potential of its air-cooled, six-cylinder engine." So where did that leave the Mustang and Barracuda? "Excepting the Corvair, they're the best of their kind."

Of course, the car-buying public saw things a little differently....

---

the 225-bhp engine. *Motor Trend* finally tested a 225-bhp GT convertible in June '66; even with Cruise-O-Matic, it managed 0-60 in a respectable 9.5 seconds, and a 17.0-second quarter mile at 81 mph.

The hydraulic-lifter 289 still rumbles powerfully at idle, throbbing through the clutch and shifter. Intake howl and a ripping exhaust note accompany even gentle acceleration. Unfortunately, the balky transmission and touchy clutch tend to interrupt the fun. Like some flashback from the thirties, the shifter demands a deliberate rhythm and a slight hesitation in neutral, and the clutch tends to bobble as it grabs. So the Mustang goes *rrrrrush* thunk, thunk, ugh... *rrrrrush* thunk, thunk, ugh... *rrrrrush* (all the way to the speed shop, presumably, to buy a Hurst shifter).

On the other hand, it's hard to argue with results, and acceleration is plenty lively, despite the shifter. The 289 sounds deliciously powerful, and puts an enormous amount of thrust under your toes—with none of the rough-running lumpiness that can characterize high-performance mills. At full throttle it bawls like a V-8 fighter jet. How much better could the Hi-Po have been?

The fast-ratio steering gear demands serious muscle, and as the Mustang squirms into a sharp corner, rolling and plowing, the tightly-wound steering wants to straighten out. A gentle application of the throttle, however, effectively erases the understeer and slithers the 'Stang round the bend. It's a lot of work, but a lot of fun, too, and it kept me distracted from the GT's stiff ride.

Fortunately, the pedals are placed perfectly for heel-and-toe downshifts. The brakes feel firm and strong, and don't require that much effort, considering they are non-assisted discs.

Sure, you can nit-pick these early Mustangs; cynics have been doing just that for 34 years now. But if they lacked refinement, well, at least they sold for a workaday price. And if certain individual styling features were truly awful, the overall look has held up just fine for more than three decades. With the original '65-66 Mustang, Ford put a lot of individuality and fun into more than a million garages and driveways—and that has to count for something.

History & Background

There was no 1964½ Mustang, at least not according to Ford. Dearborn indeed debuted its pioneering pony on April 17, 1964, but from the start referred to it as

a *1965* model. Still, Mustangs built after August 17, 1964, differ from the "early" '65s assembled before that date. Some of the changes were trivial, such as plated rather than color-keyed door lock buttons, Allen screws rather than clips to attach the inside door handles, and a wire bale to keep the fuel filler cap from wandering once removed. The Mustang nameplate on the front fender expanded from 4.75 inches to a full five inches long. Somewhat more significant was an adjustable passenger seat, an improved battery, and a switch from a generator to an alternator, with a corresponding change to the appropriate idiot light on the dashboard.

But far more relevant (and interesting) was the rapid expansion of the Mustang option list that occurred during the extended model year.

Top: *Grille-mounted fog lamps were also part of GT package.* ***Above:*** *Backup lamps ride below bumper, as on other Mustangs.*

Even the engine lineup changed. Original choices consisted of a 101-bhp, 170-c.i.d. six; a 164-bhp, 260-c.i.d. V-8; and a 210-bhp, 289-c.i.d. V-8. Sixes came with a three-speed floor shift synchronized on the top two gears, and offered Cruise-O-Matic or an English Ford four-speed as options. V-8's came with "Synchro-Smooth Drive," an all-synchronized three speed; Cruise-O-Matic or a home-grown four-speed were optional.

The Inevitable Comparison, Part II

	Corvair Corsa	Tempest GTO*	Barracuda	Mustang 2+2
Price as tested	$3,230	$3,964	$3,344	$3,696
Engine	Flat-6	V-8	V-8	V-8
Bore x stroke, in.	3.44 x 2.94	4.06 x 3.75	3.63 x 3.31	4.00x2.87
C.i.d.	164	389	273	289
Compression	8.0:1**	10.75:1	10.5:1	10.5:1
Bhp @ rpm	180 @ 4,000	325 @ 4,800	235 @ 5,200	271 @ 6000
Torque (lb-ft) @ rpm	232 @ 3,200	428 @ 3,200	280 @ 4,000	312 @ 3400
Transmission	4-speed	4-speed	4-speed	4-speed
Axle ratio	3.55:1	3.23:1	3.55:1	3.89:1
Wheelbase, in.	108	115	106	108
Curb weight, lb.	2,540	3,360	3,170	3,000
Performance				
0-60 mph, seconds	10.0	7.7	8.0	7.6
40-60 mph, seconds	7.1	na	3.7	4.0
50-70 mph, seconds	5.0	na	4.8	3.8
1/4 mile @ mph	18.1 @ 79	15.8 @ 93	16.1 @ 87	15.9 @ 89
Max speed, mph (obs)	114	115	110	114
Braking, 60-0 ft.	146.0	183.0	164.5	150.0

*1964 model
**turbocharged

The numbers above, taken from the January 1965 issue of *Motor Trend*, illustrate in objective terms how the Mustang fastback compared against its closest competitors. The Hi-Po Mustang clearly beat the hottest possible Corvair and Barracuda for raw acceleration—although the turbocharged Corvair (somewhat to our surprise) equaled the Mustang's top speed. Then, just because we enjoy this kind of thing, we added a Pontiac GTO to the fray—a convertible with a single four-barrel that *MT* tested in January '64. Bigger-engined, more powerful, but also heavier, the Goat beat the Pony, but not by all that much. Why a '64 GTO? Because we couldn't find a test of a four-speed '65. But the automatic-transmission '65 sampled by *MT* turned in a 0-60 time of 7.2 seconds, a quarter mile in 16.1 seconds at 89 mph, and a maximum speed of 115—all very comparable to the four-speed, high-output Mustang.

specifications

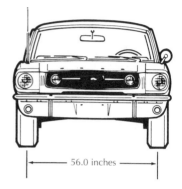

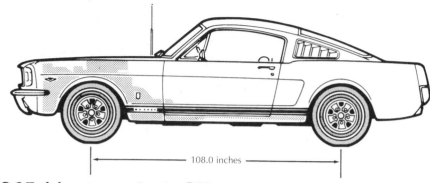

56.0 inches

108.0 inches

1965 Mustang 2+2 GT

Base price, Mustang 2+2	$2,589
Std. equip. includes	Heater/defroster, sun visors, carpeting, vinyl bucket seats, seat belts, padded dash
GT package adds	Front disc brakes, fog lights, handling package, dual exhausts, lower body stripe
Options on dR car	225-bhp V-8, 4-speed transmission, interior decor group, console, AM radio, deluxe steering wheel, remote outside mirror, day/night inside mirror, Rally Pac gauges, styled-steel wheels, engine dress-up kit
Price as equipped (est)	$3,600

ENGINE
Type	V-8
Bore x stroke	4.00 inches x 2.87 inches
Displacement	289 cubic inches
Compression ratio	10.0:1
Horsepower @ rpm	225 @ 4,800
Torque @ rpm	305 @ 3,200
Taxable horsepower	51.2
Valve gear	Ohv
Valve lifters	Hydraulic
Main bearings	5
Induction system	1 Autolite 4-bbl downdraft
Fuel system	Mechanical pump
Lubrication system	Pressure, gear-type pump
Cooling system	Pressure, centrifugal pump
Exhaust system	Dual
Electrical system	12-volt

TRANSMISSION
Type	4-speed manual, all synchronized
Ratios: 1st	2.78:1
2nd	1.93:1
3rd	1.36:1
4th	1.00:1
Reverse	2.78:1

CLUTCH
Type	Single dry plate
Diameter	10.4 inches

DIFFERENTIAL
Type	Hypoid, semi-floating
Ratio	3.00:1

STEERING
Type	Recirculating ball
Turns lock-to-lock	3.5
Ratios	16.0:1 gear; 21.7:1 overall
Turning circle	38.0 feet (curb/curb)

BRAKES
Type	4-wheel hydraulic
Front	10-inch vented disc
Rear	10-inch drum
Swept area	345 square inches
Parking brake	Mechanical, on rear wheels

CHASSIS & BODY
Construction	Platform frame with integral body
Body	Welded steel stampings
Body style	2+2 fastback coupe

SUSPENSION
Front	Independent, upper A-arms, lower strut-stabilized arms, coil springs, link-type anti-roll bar
Rear	Live axle on asymmetric leaf springs, compression shackles at rear

Shock absorbers	Hydraulic, telescopic (front); hydraulic, telescopic, diagonal-mounted (rear)
Tires	Goodyear Power Cushion 6.95 x 14
Wheels	14 x 5.0-inch stamped steel disc

WEIGHTS AND MEASURES
Wheelbase	108 inches
Overall length	181.6 inches
Overall width	68.2 inches
Overall height	51.1 inches
Front track	56.0 inches
Rear track	56.0 inches
Ground clearance	5.2 inches
Weight (w/o options)	2,621 pounds
Weight as equipped	2,960 pounds (est.)

CAPACITIES
Crankcase	5 quarts
Transmission	4.0 pints
Rear axle	4.5 pints
Cooling system	14.5 quarts (with heater)
Fuel tank	16 gallons

CALCULATED DATA
Bhp per c.i.d.	0.78
Stroke/bore	0.72
Lb./bhp	13.2
Lb./sq. in. of swept brake area	8.6

Right: *Rally Pac gauges are a compromise at best. They're mounted on steering column rather than designed into dash.* **Facing page, top:** *Good-looking side vent treatment is reminiscent of Italian GT cars of the sixties.* **Center:** *Dual exhausts exit below bumper.* **Below:** *Mustang retained center-mount fuel filler for years.*

1965 Mustang

In June '64, Ford released a 271-bhp "High Performance" 289 with the same solid-lifter cam and big-bore carb as the 289 Cobra. This engine was mated exclusively to its own Ford-built, close-ratio four-speed transmission. The Hi-Po's $442.60 price tag also included stiffer springs (by about 28 percent, front and rear), re-valved shocks, a bigger front anti-roll bar, fast-ratio steering and, originally, 6.50 x 14 tires with 5.90 x 15's offered optionally. Buyers of less potent V-8 Mustangs could order the same chassis package for $30.64.

Road & Track found the 289/271 entirely tractable at anything over 1,000 rpm; staffers even acquired the lazy habit of skipping two close ratios and shifting from first directly into fourth. The handling package reduced (but did not quite eliminate) both understeer and the Mustang's tendency to steer right under hard acceleration. "There is a certain amount of harshness to the ride at low speeds over poor surfaces," the *R&T* testers continued, "but this is a small price to pay for the great improvement in handling and road holding.... The effect is to eliminate the wallow we experienced with previous Mustangs, and to tie the car to the road more firmly, so that in a fast turn, the point of one's departure into the boondocks is delayed very considerably."

Another change came in July, when Ford modified the optional dual exhaust system, replacing the single transverse muffler with dual resonators.

Then, with the end of "early '65" pro-

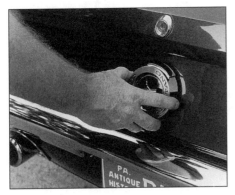

duction on August 17, a 120-bhp, 200-c.i.d., seven-main-bearing six replaced the Falcon-derived 170 as the Mustang's base engine. A two-barrel 289, producing 200 bhp, replaced the 260 as the base V-8. Higher-compression heads boosted the four-barrel 289 from 210 to 225 bhp. The 271-bhp 289 continued unchanged, but all handling-package cars were upgraded with 6.95 x 14 Red Line rubber, and the 15-inch wheels were dropped entirely.

And then there was the lovely Mustang Fastback 2+2—a car created on a whim, approved on a hunch, and nurtured by the enthusiasm that surrounded the entire Mustang project.

Mike Lamm has already recounted the Mustang's origin in admirable detail (see *SIA* #24), so we'll repeat only the relevant highlights here. Lee A. Iacocca had barely turned 35 in November 1960, when Henry Ford II appointed him vice president and general manager of the Ford Division. By early '61, Lido was busy scribbling private notes about the need for a youth-oriented product to enliven Ford's then-conservative image. He broached the idea to Marketing Manager Chase Morsey, Jr. and Product Planning Manager Donald N. Frey. Frey, in turn, involved Ford styling chief Gene Bordinat. Around August 2, 1962, these principals met to decide just what kind of car they ought to build. They decided on a four-seater based on the Falcon mechanical package, and set price and weight targets of $2,500 and 2,500 pounds (which the engineering team, headed by Executive Engineer Jack Prendergast, beat in both cases).

One more critical decision was reached, even at this early stage. An unusually wide range of options would allow buyers to custom-tailor the new car to their own whim and purpose.

Later on, Iacocca would speak of "the three faces of Mustang." Depending on options, the car could be basic, practical transportation with a little sporty flair; a luxurious mini-Thunderbird; or a real performance machine. Or, to some extent, a mix-and-match combination of all of the above.

Initial market research surveys had shown buyer preference equally divided between notchback and fastback body styles. But of the seven full-size clays presented to management on August 16, 1962, it was a notchback—the so-called "Cougar," created by Joe Oros with Dave Ash, Gale Halderman, and others—that won the hearts of both Iacocca and Hank the Deuce. Approved in early September, that car evolved into the definitive Mustang hardtop by mid-December. Still, Bordinat ordered a fastback version on his own initiative, and kept it secret until he was ready to show Iacocca in May 1963.

Bordinat's group began sketching the fastback in February '63. They considered variations with and without quarter windows, with opening rear hatches and folding rear seats. One rather bizarre drawing, perhaps inspired by the Thunderbird Sports Roadster, proposed an internal tonneau cover fitted between and behind the front buckets, sealing off

Above: Optional 225-horsepower V-8 provides plenty of poke to 3,000-pound Ford. ***Below left:*** Vent treatment is just as handsome inside car. ***Right:*** Pony interior package includes these embossed equines.

the entire rear seating area. Ultimately, the designers settled on a blind-quarter roofline that arched over the driver and then plunged down to the rear deck, where it met a short but conventional trunk opening. The full-scale model shown to management on May 2 looked exactly like the production car, save for the "caged cougar" in its grille and "Cougar" script at the forward end of its front fenders.

Later, Bordinat told historian Gary Witzenburg that the fastback had been "an emotional binge only," not based on "prudent analysis or a damned thing.... We had worked up such a head of steam on that first Mustang that we were already looking for variations on the theme." Iacocca approved it the moment he saw it—based on his own gut reaction, no doubt.

Once the "Mustang" label had been nailed down for the series (The designers liked "Cougar," but Ford had already previewed the horsy name on two widely publicized, and much admired, show cars), the marketing team batted around potential badges for the fastback, including GT, GTO(!), Limited,

Modified, and Grand Sport. They ultimately settled on "2+2," an honest assessment of the model's compromised rear seating. (Front-fender nameplates actually said "Mustang 2+2," while sales literature referred alternately to the "2+2" and "Fastback 2+2.") Production Fastbacks featured color-keyed headliners and sun visors (which were white on hardtops), as well as Silent-Flo ventilation, said to extract stale air through the prominent louvers in the C-pillars. The 10-square-foot rear window came with a standard tint.

One memorable brochure photo, brightly lit from inside the car and shot through the tinted backlight, showed an elegantly dressed young woman sitting sideways in the back seat. The caption read "rear seat luxury in the 2+2." The woman was smiling, but not convincingly; she looked uncomfortable. The 2+2 also surrendered trunk space to the hardtop, with only five cubic feet against the notchback's nine. But the Fastback's rear seat folded neatly out of sight, leaving a 35 x 41-inch platform for another 18.5 cubic feet of luggage.

Ford officially unveiled the 2+2 on

September 9, 1964, and released it for sale on September 25. Customers were already waiting six weeks for hardtops and convertibles.

And the new options kept on coming. Disc brakes by Kelsey-Hayes, promised from the beginning, finally trickled into production. Ford had first installed discs on the '63 Falcon Sprint, after Holman and Moody had warned that a V-8-powered, drum-braked Falcon would never make it around the turns at Monte Carlo.

The disc brakes, the new body style, and the high-output motor transformed the Mustang. "It has a long, sleek profile and very harmonious proportions," commented *Car and Driver* in October. "The new fastback Mustang fitted with the 'handling package'...disc brakes on the front wheels, and the high-performance version of the 289 V-8 is more closely comparable to a full-house Corvette than anything else in the Ford stable."

In April—just in time for the Mustang's first birthday—Ford released the Interior Decor Group, known today as the "pony interior" because of the running horses embossed on the seats. Beside these more elaborately styled vinyl buckets, the package also included molded carpeting, unique inner doors with courtesy lights and integral arm rests, a five-dial instrument pod with gauges for amps and oil pressure in addition to the standard temperature and fuel level, and simulated walnut panels on the dash and (if ordered) console. Sun visors were padded and color-keyed, and the pedals chrome-trimmed. Even the door handles and window cranks were unique. Promoted with the

Group, but actually offered as a separate option, was a lovely wood-grain steering wheel.

Also in April, Ford put all the chassis goodies together in the new GT package. Available with the 225-bhp 289 with three-speed, four-speed, or automatic transmission—or with 271-bhp Hi-Po and a four-speed—the GT group included the handling package and front disc brakes plus driving lights in the grille and dual exhausts that boldly stabbed through the rocker panels, terminating in boldly flared chrome trumpets. "And running front to rear along the lower body," enthused a Mustang brochure, "is the triple stripe that Ford's GT racing car carries in European competition!" Inside, GT's sported the same five-dial instrument pod as Interior Decor cars, but set in a black rather than wood-grain background. (Mustangs with both the Interior Decor and GT packages had wood grain.)

GT production had actually begun in February. Ford offered the package on all three Mustang body styles, although most promotional photos showed it on the 2+2. Of course, the model year was almost over then, and Ford produced only 15,079 Mustang GT's for 1965. Mustang owners themselves probably cobbled together a few more. Dealers offered the grille, lights, and exhaust system at the parts counter, and a November '65 magazine ad urged owners to "Make your Mustang into a GT! Your Ford Dealer has the goods."

In 1966, the first full model year for the GT package, Ford sold another 25,517 examples. ☞

Acknowledgments and Bibliography

Books: John A. Gunnell, Mustang, the Affordable Sportscar, *and* Standard Catalog of American Cars 1946-1975; *F. Wilson McComb,* Ford Mustang; *Peter C. Sessler,* Mustang Red Book; *Gary L. Witzenburg,* Mustang, the Complete History of America's Pioneer Ponycar.

Periodicals: L. Scott Bailey, "Bertone Builds a Mustang," Automobile Quarterly, Vol. 4, No. 2; David E. Davis, Jr., "Making the inevitable comparison..." Car and Driver, October 1964; Steve Kelly, "Mustangs!", Motor Trend, June 1966; Michael Lamm, "First Mustang," SIA #24; Bob McVay, "Mustang 2+2 Road Test," Motor Trend, January 1965; Stephen F. Wilder, "Mustang by Bertone," Road & Track, January 1966; "Road Research Report: Ford Mustang," Car and Driver, May 1964; "A More Muscular Mustang," Road & Track, September 1964; "Ford Mustang," Car and Driver, October 1964; "Special Mustang Edition," Car Life, 1965.

Thanks to Kim M. Miller of the AACA Library and Research Center; Henry Siegle; and of course special thanks to owner Nelson Grossnickle.

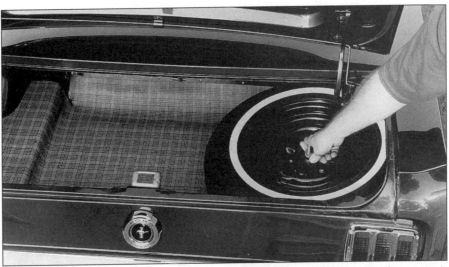

Above: Spare squeezes available trunk space. *Below:* Rear passengers sit low; area is more useful when converted to cargo carrier. *Bottom left:* Rally Pac consists of tach and this 24-hour clock. *Right:* Rear-seat release hides in trunk.

Scoopology

The Mustang show car that debuted at Watkins Glen in the fall of 1962 was powered by a mid-mounted V-4, cooled by huge, horizontally louvered scoops just behind the doors. Such an intake would of course have no function on a front-engine car, but the Ford designers rather liked it, and so they worked a long, scoop-like indentation into the side of the production Mustang. (Ford's mid-engine GT-40 race cars sported a somewhat similar, albeit functional, arrangement, but were developed *after* the Mustang theme had been approved.)

On most Mustangs, this indentation led to a chrome-plated vertical slash that simulated an actual air intake. From the start, however, Ford offered a $27.11 "Accent Group" that deleted the chrome bauble in favor of a pin stripe around the entire indentation. Ford also left the

chrome piece off *all* Fastbacks. The full-scale model that Iacocca approved in May '63 didn't have it, and that's the way the body style went to production—although 2+2 buyers could still order the Accent Group pinstripe for $13.60. Mustang GTs, regardless of body style, also lacked the chrome scoop.

Aside from the new "floating horse" grille, the most noticeable change in the '66 Mustang was a more elaborate fender scoop, with three short horizontal spears projecting forward out of the "opening." But '66 GTs, 2+2s, and Accent Group cars still wore their quarter-panels plain, making them difficult to distinguish from '65s. 1966 GTs are particularly hard to spot, as they retained the '65 GT grille and driving lights. In fact, the only visual change between a '65 and '66 GT is the more prominent horse-and-bars emblem on the '66 gas cap.

Hertz's Rent-A-Racer

RENTAL car ads really slay me. They go on ad nauseam reciting the advantages of renting from this company or that, promulgating their messages through the mouths of well-known athletes and actors who in truth know nothing about the rental car business. But all the hoopla is effective; the ads leave one with the distinct impression that the future course of his or her life will be irreversibly altered if a rental form is signed with one of "the other" companies. To further drive home their point, the marketing types have devised "clubs" to make harried travelers feel as though they're really part of a big happy family of car renters.

But what Hertz, Avis, National, Budget, et al fail to mention is that regardless of the name on the rental contract, you're going to be driving the same type of boring econobox, propelled by four tiny cylinders feeding their output through a reluctant automatic transmission. (Unless of course, you opt to step up to the excitement of a V-6, which is to be found in some of the models available at a significantly higher cost.) They may be able to get you through the airport as though you've been shot from a cannon, but once you hit the freeway, you'll have to pedal to maintain much over 55 mph.

But the rental car fleets were not always inhabited solely by jejune automotive creations; in the mid-1960s, Hertz one-upped the competition by offering pukka sports cars to the renting public. It was done under the banner of the Hertz Sports Car Club, which was, in fact, open to anyone over 25 with a valid driver's license. With the burgeoning interest in performance that marked the mid and late sixties, the concept of renting sports cars was a stroke of genius.

The Hertz Sports Car Club's first offering was none other than Chevrolet's finest—the Corvette. But in 1965, the company began renting "Fords and other fine cars" and with the move away from General Motors, the sports car program appeared to be in trouble. Not to worry. The folks at Shelby-American soon came to the rescue. According to Rick Kopec in his *Shelby American*

by Dave Emanuel
photos by the author

Guide, Carroll Shelby and Shelby-American general manager Peyton Cramer capitalized on Hertz's switch in automaker allegiance by proposing that the company substitute Shelby Mustangs for Corvettes. "Cramer approached Hertz with the idea that they offer a special edition black-and-gold GT-350H —available only through Hertz—to their Hertz Sports Car Club members. Cramer and Shelby had envisioned a contract of, perhaps 25 or 50 cars, but Hertz ate the idea up. Cramer walked away from the meeting with an order for 1000 cars!"

Knowing car renters as I do, and as I imagine Hertz did, it is amazing that the company chose to place unmodified Shelby GT-350s in its fleet. With no financial responsibility for any repair bills that might arise from "cruel and unusual" treatment, many car renters immediately become aspiring race drivers upon slipping behind the wheel of even the most lackluster vehicle—one can only imagine what they would do with a high powered car that had excellent handling characteristics. Yet that's precisely what they got when they plunked down $17.00 per day to rent a Shelby.

There was considerably more to trans-

forming a Mustang to GT-350 than applying racing stripes and cosmetic touches; a not inconsequential amount of engine and chassis rework was performed before the completed cars rolled out of Shelby-American's Los Angeles Airport facility. Since the cars were originally intended to challenge early Corvettes and XK-E Jaguars in SCCA's B/Production sports car class, Carroll Shelby had devised a package that offered enthusiasts the bare bones of a race car. Although special competition versions were also produced, a standard GT-350 could be successfully raced with relatively few modifications. In fact, a *Sports Car Graphic* road test reported, "At one point in the track testing we had the car at Riverside and in completely street trim were able to bomb through certain parts of the course including the esses at speeds higher than many all-out racing cars can be run through."

Although to the casual observer, the Shelby GT-350 and standard 2 plus 2 Mustang appear so similar as to be almost identical, the cars share little in common beyond sheet metal. Not content with the 271-horsepower rating of Ford's high performance 289 V-8 engine, Shelby added a 715 cfm Holley four-barrel with center-pivot float bowls, high rise aluminum "Cobra" intake manifold, tubular exhaust headers (which fed into straight-through mufflers), finned aluminum rocker arm covers and oil pan. These changes brought horsepower up to 306 at 6000 rpm with a corresponding torque rating of 329 lbs/ft at 4200 rpm.

In place of the standard Ford four-speed transmission, Shelby selected an aluminum cased Borg-Warner close-ratio gearbox with a 2.36:1 first gear, 1.62:1 second, 1.20:1 third and 1:1 fourth. A heavy duty 10.5-inch diameter Ford clutch served to interface engine and transmission. The remainder of the driveline consisted of a hefty live rear axle assembly which was a shortened version of the one used in the full-sized Ford Galaxie. A 3.89:1 axle ratio with a "No-Spin" (also known as a "Detroit Locker") limited slip differential was standard.

Originally published in Special Interest Autos #78, Nov.-Dec. 1983

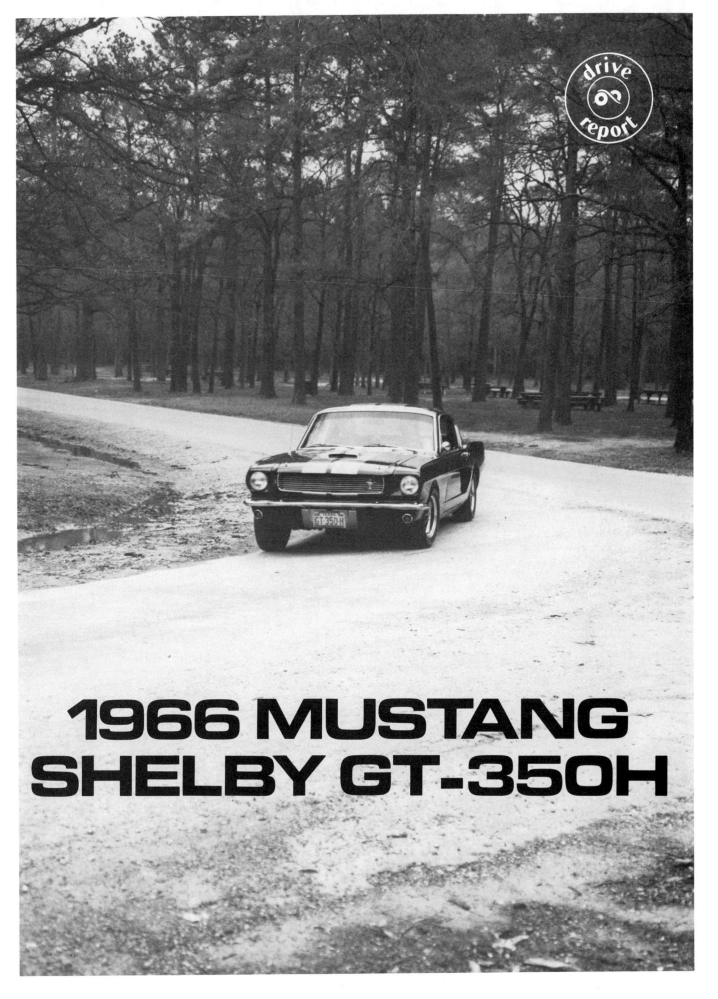

1966 MUSTANG SHELBY GT-350H

*Right: All steel hood with stripes derived from GT-350 was used on H model. **Below:** Bold graphic ID preceded rocker stripes on each side of car. **Far right:** Rear brake cooling scoops were new for 1966. **Bottom:** Styled steel wheels carried Cobra emblems.*

1966 MUSTANG

These modifications certainly perked up the Mustang's performance, but it was Shelby's suspension alterations that provided the GT-350 with a personality all its own. In order to allow the front wheels to remain more nearly vertical while the car was being shuttled through a high speed turn, Shelby lowered the inner pivot point of the upper A-arms one inch. This also served to raise the front roll center, thereby reducing understeer. To further neutralize the standard Mustang's tendency to plow, front anti-sway bar diameter was increased from .84 inch to 1.0 inch. An "export" (so named because it was included on Mustangs intended for

overseas delivery) brace, connecting each spring tower to the firewall and a "Monte Carlo" bar (its name derives from the fact that a similar device was used on Falcons driven in the previous year's Monte Carlo rally) were also included to reduce front end flex under load.

At the rear, semi-elliptic leaf springs functioned in combination with a pair of stout torque reaction bars located above the axle and anchored to the chassis inside the passenger compartment. Koni adjustable shock absorbers were used at all four corners as were 5½-inch x 15-inch steel wheels (15 x 6 Shelby designed, Cragar built wheels with cast aluminum center and steel rim were optional at $273) and 775-15 Goodyear Blue Dot tires. Shelby also quickened the steering ratio from 27:1 to 19:1 (with a corresponding

reduction from 5.0 to 3.75 in number of lock to lock turns) by lengthening the Pitman and idler arms.

Although the Shelby-wrought changes produced a vehicle that handled and accelerated immeasurably better than a stock Mustang, they did so at the expense of comfort. According to *Road & Track*, "The ride of the GT-350 would have to rate as poor if comfort were the main consideration. The springs, though comparatively soft, are snubbed by the stiff shock settings and an abrupt dip results in thunking at both ends. On glass-smooth turns, the GT-350 is very fast, the considerable body lean not at all disconcerting to the driver, and a cornering attitude can be maintained with the throttle. The most effective technique for a slow turn seems to be to wait late, brake hard, shift down, point the nose toward the apex and push it around with the throttle. This is easily controlled in the GT-350, even when the rear end begins to go and it's time to feather back a bit to keep the car aimed in the right direction. Past the apex, winding off, the GT-350 will take a surprising amount of throttle without losing its balance.

"Over rough paving, the cornering technique is altogether different as the combination of power, mass and stiff suspension demands a very delicate touch. The rear end, which carries only 45 percent of the car's weight, even after all the changes which were made, is inclined to lose its poise on rough surfaces and changes in throttle opening must be made with extreme care if embarrassment is to be avoided."

In all, 562 GT-350s were sold during the 1965 model year. Such a sales volume is inconsequential by Detroit standards, but it represented a re-

sounding success for Shelby-American, whose primary raison d'etre was to homologate the cars for competition in SCCA's Production category. However, Shelby, with a slight assist from Ford management, realized that sales would have been significantly higher if the GT-350 had sacrificed some race worthiness for improved road manners. So in 1966, a new course was charted.

Some 1966 models were actually leftovers from the previous year, so they contained many of the traits that were eliminated later in the model year. (According to Rick Kopec's *Shelby Buyer's Guide*, 252 leftover 1965 cars were converted to 1966 models.) Due largely to dealer reports and Ford corporate evaluation, the '66 Shelby was revised to broaden its market appeal and lower production costs (the latter being most conducive to broadening appeal). Alterations included plexiglass rear windows in place of the standard Mustang vents, side scoops that funneled air to the rear brakes, a folding rear seat (the '65 model contained a rear shelf on which the spare tire was mounted, rather than a seat), revised dashboard and 14-inch rather than 15-inch diameter wheels. Relocation of the front "A" arms was eliminated and the over-axle traction bars were replaced by an easier to install type that bolted beneath the axle. Since the lock-up and disengagement action of the "Detroit Locker" differential was rather noisy, it was moved to the option list for 1966, as were the Koni shock absorbers. Other new options for the year included an automatic transmission and a variety of exterior colors; while all '65s were white,

1966 models could be ordered in white, green, black, blue and red.

For a variety of reasons, not the least of which was undoubtedly maintenance expense, Hertz did not continue the GT-350H program in 1967. However, in 1968, 1969 and 1970 the company did include a number of standard (not special Hertz versions) Shelby GT-350s in its rental fleet. Having learned a costly lesson in 1966, all the 1968 and later cars were equipped with automatic transmissions. The decision to revive the rent-a-Shelby program was based in part on the general softening of the cars. With the debut of the 1968 model, the high performance, mechanical lifter equipped 289 disappeared from the scene. It was replaced by a mild 302 engine rated at 250 horsepower. Save for an aluminum intake manifold, Holley 600 CFM four-barrel, "Cobra" valve covers and air filter, these engines were identical to those installed in standard Ford products. These cars, being easy to drive and offering a comfortable ride, were obviously successful as profitable rental vehicles as Hertz kept them in its fleet for three years—until Shelby-American ceased vehicle

production.

With the 1967 introduction of the GT-500, the smaller engined 350 lost most of its thunder. By 1968 it had become little more than a cosmetic package suited for buyers in quest of the Shelby image as opposed to true high performance. A good thing had come to an end. But it was certainly fun while it lasted.

Driving Impressions

Hertz management knew a good thing when it smacked them in the face, and they committed approximately $300,000 to advertise the availability of the Shelby GT-350H. Ads began with such unabashed headlines as, "There are only 1000 of these for rent in the entire world. Hertz has them all." They went on to state, "It's the Shelby GT-350H. Only Hertz rents it. Cobra engine. Disc brakes. High speed wheels and tires. Stick shift or automatic. Rally stripes. High performance shocks. Torque controlled rear axle. The whole load. Why a rent-a-car with all this performance? We could have gotten a fleet of high-powered pseudo-sports-cars. But we

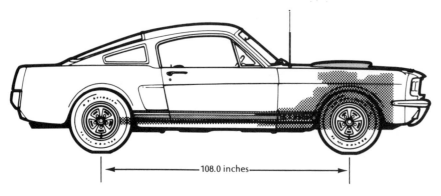

108.0 inches | 57.0 inches

1966 Mustang Shelby GT-350H

Price	$17.00 per day plus 17¢ per mile
Optional equipment	None

ENGINE

Type	V-8 ohv
Bore & stroke	4.00 inches x 2.87 inches
Displacement	289 cubic inches
Bhp @ rpm	306 @ 6000 rpm
Torque @ rpm	329 at 4200 rpm
Compression ratio	10.0:1
Induction	Ford/Autolite 4-bbl on "Cobra" aluminum intake manifold
Exhaust system	Tubular headers, straight-through glass-packed mufflers
Electrical system	12-volt battery/coil

TRANSMISSION

Type	3-speed automatic
Ratios: 1st	2.46:1
2nd	1.46:1
3rd	1:1
Reverse	2.20:1

DIFFERENTIAL

Type	Hypoid semi-floating
Ratio	3.89:1

STEERING

Type	Semi-reversible, recirculating ball, power assisted
Ratio	19.1:1
Turns lock to lock	3.75
Turning circle	38 feet

BRAKES

Type	Hydraulic, Kelsey Hayes, 11.3-inch diameter ventilated front discs, 10.0-inch x 2.5-inch rear drums
Total swept area	381 square inches

CHASSIS & BODY

Construction	Welded platform with boxed side rails
Body	2-door coupe

SUSPENSION

Front	Independent SLA, coil springs, double-acting tubular shocks, 1.0-inch anti-sway bar
Rear	Live axle with 4-leaf semi-elliptic springs, double acting shocks, torque control arms
Wheels	14-inch x 6-inch styled steel
Tires	6.95 x 14 low profile nylon

DIMENSIONS

Wheelbase	108.0 inches
Overall length	181.6 inches
Overall height	55 inches
Overall width	68.2 inches
Front tread	57 inches
Rear tread	57 inches
Curb weight	2790 pounds

PERFORMANCE

Maximum speed	132 mph
Acceleration: 0-60	6.9 seconds
Standing start ¼-mile	14.8 seconds and 96 mph
Fuel economy	11-15 mpg. Premium required

1966 MUSTANG

figured you'd want to try a champion. Not just another imitation. So we got the one car that holds the Sports Car Club of America National Championship." Yes, this is the same company that now equates excitement with O.J. Simpson running through airport lobbies.

The first cars inducted into the Hertz program were actually 1965 models caught on the Shelby production line during model year change-over. Although they were released as 1966 vehicles, they were blessed with 1965 mechanicals including four-speed transmission, Detroit Locker differential, over-axle traction bars and lowered "A"-arm pivot points. I wondered if anybody at the time realized what they were getting for $17.00 a day and 17 cents

For $17 a day and 17¢ per mile, Hertz gave you blindingly fast performance.

Left: 289 Cobra engine develops more than one hp per cubic inch. Below left: Tach is redlined at seven grand. Below: Fold-down rear seat was a $75 Shelby-American option. Below center: Shelby's ID appears on scuff plates. Bottom: Plastic rear window inserts were new for 1966 on GT-350 cars.

per mile—here was a car that could be run in SCCA competition with the simple addition of a roll bar. Evidently, that thought occurred to more than one renter back in 1966. Hertz reportedly found traces of roll bar mountings in more than one car indicating that the rent-a-racer slogan had been taken literally.

Initially, all the Hertz cars were painted black and had "Bronze Power Gold" LeMans stripes running from the splash shield below the front bumper, up over the hood, top and deck lid, terminating at the bottom of the valance panel below the rear bumper. Additionally, gold stripes with "GT-350H" at the front were painted on the rocker panels. Later in the year, Hertz cars were produced in the full complement of 1966 colors and the LeMans stripes were occasionally deleted.

As might be expected, it didn't take long before complaints of slipping clutches became excessive. It's questionable whether the malady arose from outright abuse or uneducated left feet, but the end result was that Hertz quickly switched to cars equipped with Ford's high performance C-4 automatic. As with non-Hertz Shelbys, when an automatic transmission was fitted, a Ford Autolite carburetor took the place of the Holley four-barrel used in conjunction with the four-speed.

Another change made to many Hertz cars concerned the master cylinder. Higher-than-normal pedal effort was required to slow or stop the cars, prompting a number of customer complaints alleging faulty brakes. In fact, the brakes were functioning perfectly—the need for excessive pedal pressure arose from lack of a power booster and use of special heavy duty type front pads and rear shoes. To alleviate the problem, Hertz installed special master cylinders on

Below: Model ID is also displayed on rear panel. Right: There's plenty of rear visibility to see the rest of the traffic falling behind you. Bottom: The car handles very well at high speeds.

1966 MUSTANG

many cars. This did lower the pedal effort required, but Hertz retained a special warning label advising, "This vehicle is equipped with competition brakes. Heavier than normal pedal pressure is required."

While some (early) GT-350H cars rode on 15-inch wheels, the overwhelming majority received 14-inch x 6-inch styled steel, "Magnum 500" wheels produced by Motor Wheel Corporation. These were similar to the standard GT-350 wheels, the difference being the wheels bolted onto Hertz cars had chromed rather than painted spokes. Some vehicles were also fitted with wheel center caps imprinted with "Hertz Sports Car Club" rather than "GT-350."

Like many early Shelbys, "H" models and otherwise, the car shown here, belonging to Brian Poe of Houston, Texas, had been modified from its original configuration. When Poe purchased the car, a four-speed transmission was in residence and several other incorrect pieces had been installed. But today, the car is largely correct as initially produced and

delivered to Hertz. It is also driven on a regular basis.

Upon first climbing behind the wheel, I realized why these cars had and continue to have such great appeal. Even with automatic transmission, an early GT-350 comes off as a no-nonsense performance vehicle. Fitted with neither power steering nor power brakes, driving is a very physical experience. I hate to use the term "man's car," but that description is most adequate—one must possess a degree of brute strength to feel comfortable when turning the wheel or stabbing the brake pedal. This is not a car for the effete of mind or body.

Another item certain to put some drivers off is the extremely stiff suspension. Even with wide bias/belted tires, the car comes unstuck a bit too easily when thrown around on rough pavement. This problem isn't unique to the GT-350; it is a concern when any vehicle with competition-type suspension is driven on city streets. It's simply the price one pays in owning a car with a racing heritage. On the other hand, a dividend is awarded in terms of handling on smoother surfaces. The Shelby can be bent around corners with little body roll and excellent controllability. Having a lightweight 289 powerplant beneath the hood, early Shelbys demon-

strate much better balance than later models.

The exceptionally responsive engine is surprisingly docile considering that it is producing over one horsepower per cubic inch. Although the mechanical lifters quite definitely make their presence known, their characteristic clatter isn't at all objectionable, and in fact they transmit a delightfully mechanical whirring sound to discerning ears in the passenger compartment. However, the camshaft's generous valve timing requires an idle speed of 800-1000 rpm which causes a rather pronounced clunk when the transmission is pulled from Neutral to Drive. Mitigating this is the powerplant's enthusiastic response to accelerator pedal input; it pulls so strongly from just above idle to red line as to belie its displacement of a mere 289 cubic inches. Carroll Shelby quite apparently chose all the "right stuff" in engine modifications. □

Acknowledgements and Bibliography
Road and Track, *various issues 1965-1966;* Sports Car Graphic, *various issues 1965-1966;* The Shelby American Guide, *by Richard J. Kopec;* Shelby Buyer's Guide, *by Richard J. Kopec. Our thanks to Bill Mosley. Special thanks to Brian Poe, Houston, Texas.*

Color Gallery

1964 ½ convertible

Ford's sporty Mustang was an unexpected runaway success. Ford hoped to sell 150,000 the first year. Over 121,000 1964 ½ models alone were sold. By the end of 1965, 680,989 had been built, of which 101,945 were convertibles like this 200hp, 289-cu.in Challenger V-8-powered soft-top.

1964 ½ convertible K-code

Among the most highly regarded of the early Mustangs are those with the high-performance "K-Code," 271hp, 289-cu.in. V-8. Of the 28,833 1964 ½ convertibles built, it is believed that only a handful were so optioned, as only 7,273 Mustangs received this engine during its first year and a half of production.

1965 coupe

Equipped with a minimum of options, this is a prime example of the way the majority of the early Mustangs were ordered. The base 200-cu.in., 120hp, six-cylinder, 3-speed transmission and 13-inch steel wheels made for an inexpensive, sporty-looking car and helped Ford sell over 500,000 in its first full year.

1966 coupe

A new grille with a "floating" pony in a chrome surround and chrome inserts in the side coves marked the few styling changes for 1966. Mustang's second full model year saw the highest production totals, with 499,751 of the 607,568 built being hardtop coupes like this example, powered by the base 289-cu.in. V-8 of 200hp.

Photograph by Robert Gross

1966 convertible

The epitome of an easy-cruising convertible, this soft-top was one of 72,119 built in 1966, and features a 120hp, 200-cu.in. six linked to a Cruise-O-Matic transmission, power steering and power brakes. A welcome change was the replacement of the Falcon-sourced instrument panel for one with five circular gauges.

Photograph by Robert Gross

1967 GT

Shedding its Falcon underpinnings, the 1967 Mustang was restyled, its suspension revised, and it gained the room needed to fit big engines like the 320hp, 390-cu.in. big-block V-8. The 2+2 evolved into a "true" fastback. This GT, one of 71,042 2+2s built in '67, is powered by the 271hp, 289-cu.in. and 4-speed transmission.

1968 Shelby GT500 KR

Of the 4,451 1968 Shelby Mustangs built, 1,053 were fastback GT500 KRs. These "Kings of the Road" were powered by the 428-cu.in. Cobra Jet V-8, underrated at 335 horsepower. Unlike the 1965-67 Shelbys, the '68s were built to Shelby specification by A.O. Smith Corporation in Michigan.

1968 428 Cobra Jet

Released in mid-'68, the 428-cu.in. Cobra Jet V-8 was Ford's answer to the Camaro's 396-cu.in. big-block V-8. Power front disc brakes and the GT option were required to get one of these intentionally underrated 335-hp brutes, which are regarded as the quickest Mustangs of the era. Only 1,299 CJ Mustangs were built in 1968.

Photograph by James Dietzler

1969 Mach 1 Super Cobra Jet
The 1969 Mustang was restyled, becoming longer, wider, and lower. The Mach 1 offered special striping, deluxe interior, and improved performance and handling. The Super Cobra Jet was a beefed-up 428-cu.in. V-8 Cobra Jet combined with the Drag Pack axle option. Only 13,193 1969 Mustangs were CJs or SCJs.

Photograph by Vince Wright

1969 Shelby GT 350
More road car than racer, the '69 Shelby GT350 was powered by the 290hp, 351-cu.in. V-8 and had a unique look from the Mustang, accomplished by using 21 fiberglass body parts. Shelby built 1,087 fastback GT350s in '69; 152 went to Hertz, and some were sold as 1970 models with a few cosmetic changes.

Photograph by James Dietzler

1970 Boss 429

Except for air conditioning, Ford packed as many options as possible in Boss 429s, including the NASCAR-derived, 375hp, 429-cu.in. V-8. A NASCAR homologation special, 857 were built in '69, and 499 in '70, with Kar Kraft Engineering of Michigan doing the conversions. Ford lost money on every one.

Photograph by Robert Gross

1970 Boss 302

The Mustang got a new single-headlight front end in '70; the Boss 302 added stripes, a chin spoiler, and improved suspension. A Trans Am homologation car, 7,013 Boss 302s were built in 1970. Only available with a 4-speed gearbox, its high-revving, 290hp, 302-cu.in. V-8 was revised to improve its driveability.

Photograph by James Dietzler

1971 429 Cobra Jet Mach 1
Along with a complete redesign of the Mustang came a new engine, the 370hp, 429-cu.in. Cobra Jet V-8, a one-year-only option that was installed in only 1,250 Mustangs. This big-block V-8 was the last one offered in the Mustang, and in fortified Super Cobra Jet form, was rated at 375hp.

Photograph by Robert Gross

1972 coupe
After the 1971 redesign, with its longer, wider and heavier styling, few changes were made for 1972, with the exception being that engine choices were halved, from 10 to 5. Base V-8s like this hardtop came with the 302-cu.in. V-8 of 140hp. Of the 125,093 1972 Mustangs built, some 75,000 were hardtop coupes.

1978 Mustang II King Cobra
Many Mustang fans treated the new 1974 Mustang II with scorn, but emissions and fuel economy issues made it the right car for the times. In 1978, just under 5,000 of the 192,410 IIs sold were built with the most expensive Mustang option to that time, the $1,277 King Cobra with its wild graphics and 139hp, 302-cu.in. V-8.

1973 convertible
After 1973, it would be a decade until convertible Mustangs were offered again. Little changed stylistically from '72; the grille was reworked and the front and rear bumpers slightly modified. Of the 134,867 Mustangs sold, 11,853 were soft-tops. Many, like this one, came with economical 141hp, 302-cu.in. V-8s.

© HERTZ SYSTEM, INC. 1966

There are only 1000 of these for rent in the entire world. Hertz has them all.

It's the Shelby G.T.350-H.

Only Hertz rents it.

Cobra engine. Disc brakes. High speed wheels and tires. Stick shift or automatic. Rally stripes. High performance shocks. Torque controlled rear axle. The whole load.

Why a rent-a-car with all this performance? We could have gotten a fleet of high-powered pseudo-sports-cars. But we figured you'd want to try a champion. Not just another imitation.

So we got the one car that holds the Sports Car Club of America National Championship.

And you can rent this 4-seater G.T.350-H from Hertz in most cities for a day. Or longer. But *only* from Hertz.

Two stipulations. You have to be at least 25 years old. And you have to hurry. (It's all on a first-come-first-serve basis.)

So make your reservation today. One local phone call reserves your car here. Or just about anywhere in the country.

Call the only rent-a-car company that offers you a championship G.T.350-H.

Hertz.

Let Hertz put you in the driver's seat. (Isn't that where you belong?)

49

THE ONLY BARGAIN MUSTANGS LEFT?
1966 Sprint 200

by Rick Mitchell
photos by the author

WHAT do you do after you build a million Mustangs? Start on the *second* million," Ford proclaimed to eager Mustang buyers as it kicked off its *Millionth Mustang Sale* in the spring of 1966. And to go with this special mid-year sale was an all-new model. It was equipped with wire wheel covers, a full console, chrome air cleaner cover and factory painted accent stripes. This Mustang proved to be a huge sales success that appealed to all types of buyers. Yet it was equipped with a 200-cubic-inch six engine. Its name? The 1966 *Sprint 200* Mustang.

By the latter part of 1965, Ford was suffering from a shortage of 289 V-8 engines. The 289 had become syn-onymous with the Mustang, and despite salesmen being told to "Sell the Six," too many Mustang customers were "buying the eight" instead.

A popular sales tactic at Ford was to introduce a new model at mid-year to help buyers see slower selling models in a new light. With this in mind, the company developed the Sprint package for its Mustang. By throwing on some popular goodies, Ford created the Sprint 200 Mustang. Sales of 200-cubic-inch six Mustangs soon took a giant leap forward, and the demand for V-8 models eased somewhat. At the same time, Sprint 200s were featured as "Limited Edition" models to attract added interest, and were highly promoted through

Originally published in Special Interest Autos #98, Mar.-Apr. 1987

Left: Accent paint stripes are standard, which means that side "airscoops" were omitted at factory. Below: Early Mustang trunk space is quite good, considering the short-deck styling. Bottom: Full wire wheel covers with spinners are also part of Sprint 200 package.

the *Millionth Mustang Sale.*

They were the most luxurious and economical six-cylinder first generation (1964½ to 1966) Mustangs built. Many have survived because of their solidly dependable, seven-main-bearing, six-cylinder engines, which provide peppy yet reliable performance, while delivering 20 to 24 miles per gallon on regular fuel. The 200-c.i.d. motor, which delivers 120 horsepower, is still a highly serviceable engine today, with basic tuneup components easily available.

Ford built Sprint 200 Mustangs at all three plants on the same assembly lines as the basic Mustang sixes from late November 1965 through early August 1966. But what distinguishes the Sprints from the Standard six models was the addition of the "Sprint 200 Option Group." This option came in either "Sprint Package A," with a three-speed manual transmission, or "B,"

SIA Fault Finder: 1965-66 Six-cylinder Mustangs

Three quarters of surviving Sprint 200 Mustangs are equipped with Ford's solidly dependable C-4 Cruise-O-Matic transmission. This smooth operating automatic possesses an extremely quick passing gear. Using it in an emergency rapidly kicks in a thousand hotter rpm. The other Sprints are equipped with three-speed manual transmissions which have been described as the weakest transmissions in the early Mustangs. Many owners with three speeds report needing transmission rebuilds in intervals of as few as 40,000 miles. However, both gearboxes deliver a respectable 22 to 26 miles per gallon using regular fuel.

Early six-cylinder Mustangs were designed with excellent front to rear weight ratios, giving them light to medium steering, though with a moderate amount of understeer. Most were equipped with drum brakes on both ends, requiring longer stopping distances today than what most drivers are used to.

On inspecting the interiors, one finds spacious front head and leg room. But the rear seating is considerably smaller with adequate room only for smaller children on long trips. The front seats are better padded than most

other "sporty" cars. There is excellent fresh air ventilation. Outside visibility is better than average, except in the fastback models looking towards the rear quarter panels. All 1966 Mustangs, including the sixes, used the more deluxe five-dial instrument panels. Optional Rally-Pacs were available providing a clock and tachometer.

On the downside, all early Mustangs are prone to forming rust in their lower quarter panels, rear fender wheel openings, and front fender lower doglegs. A serious problem in some is pinhole rust developing in the fresh air cowl panels allowing rainwater to leak onto the floorboards. Inspect these areas carefully!

The early Mustangs were America's first ponycars, and good, restorable six-cylinder examples are still plentiful. Better than 90 percent of the parts needed to restore one are available from Ford or reproduction companies which advertise in *SIA* or *Hemmings*. From a practical standpoint, it may well be that the most sensible car to restore today would be an early six-cylinder Mustang. They provide distinct good looks with economical performance at a reasonable price.

BARGAIN MUSTANGS

with a Cruise-O-Matic automatic transmission. With this optional package, the factory deleted the quarter panel chrome simulated intake scoops which were standard on most 1966 models, and replaced them with factory painted accent stripes highlighting the full length fender and door cutouts. Full wire-wheel covers with blue centered small spinners next replaced the standard wheelcovers. Taking the standard Mustang interior, a center console was added to every Sprint. And finally, the otherwise stock 200-cubic-inch six motor received its own special chrome air cleaner cover, an item never before seen on any previous Mustang six. On top of this was added a newly designed "Mustang Powered Sprint 200" decal. Remarkably, this extensive package of options cost only $39.63 over the base six price of $2,398.43. If "Package B" was desired with an automatic transmission, the additional price was instead only $163.40. This was a tremendous bargain considering the extras added by buying the Sprint option. It's no wonder the Sprint 200 Mustangs were so popular.

Sprint Mustangs were made in all three body styles: coupe, convertible and fastback. Although they were billed as being a "Limited Edition" model, exactly how many were made is not known. Ford did not keep separate production records to differentiate its Sprint versus standard six production totals. Sprint Mustangs were not specially coded by VIN number or data plates, and the only accurate way to verify a Sprint 200 Mustang is by its equipment. The truest indication is that if the quarter panel attaching holes for the simulated sidescoops were never drilled open at the factory, then any given 1966 six-cylinder Mustang began its life as a Sprint 200, even if all other factory Sprint equipment is missing.

Today, more and more Sprint 200 Mustangs are being revived and restored, and returned to active use. Hardtop models survive in the greatest numbers by far today, with the fastback versions being the scarcest. Some Sprints sport original factory pony interiors which greatly complement the rest of the package.

Two decades later, Sprint Mustangs are still the perfect grocery getter or second car around town. They provide excellent, reliable daily transportation. And as show cars, more Sprints are coming under the judges' eyes at collector-car and Mustang shows every year. Not only that, they're still a relative bargain to buy. □

Above: Rally-Pac of tachometer and clock was an option on Sprint 200. *Left:* Good-looking center console was standard on Sprint 200. *Below:* Ford ohv six is known to be peppy, economical and reliable.

SIA comparisonReport

1967 Mustang
versus 1967 Camaro

by Arch Brown
photos by Vince Manocchi

I 'LL tell you what Chevrolet doesn't need at the moment and that's another automobile!"

This was spoken by Semon E. "Bunkie" Knudsen, Chevy's general manager, and one can readily appreciate his point of view.

It was 1963, and the new Chevelle was just going into production, bringing to five the number of distinctly different series being offered by the division. What had prompted Knudsen's comment was a proposal that Chevrolet should develop a new, four-passenger "personal" car. Someone had likened the concept to a scaled-down version of Buick's sensationally popular and strikingly handsome new Riviera. A clay model, in fact, had actually been constructed. But after all, in addition to the forthcoming Chevelle there were the big Chevy, America's best-seller; the dashing Corvette; the economical Chevy II, and of course the Corvair. And the latter car was due to be completely reworked for 1965. Better handling, sleeker and more European in appearance, it was even available with a turbocharger for the performance-minded. What advantage could there possibly be in developing yet another "sporty" car?

Chevrolet executives were aware, of course, that Ford was well along in its development of a jaunty little number. But the new little car from Dearborn was said to be based upon Falcon components, and the Falcon was about as exciting as vanilla pudding. So what's to worry?

Even the Mustang's debut, on April 17, 1964, failed to rouse GM's corporate brass to action. Bunkie Knudsen had become a true believer by that time, but the top men at corporate headquarters remained unmoved. Jack Gordon, then president of General Motors, was a Cadillac man, conservative to the core. He wasn't about to get excited over the Mustang. Even Chevrolet's chief stylist, Irv Rybicki — who favored the idea of a new, sports-oriented Chevy — thought the little Ford was "funny looking."

The public, however, had a different reaction; 100,000 Mustangs were sold in the first four months following the car's introduction. With the exception of Lee Iacocca, hardly anybody at Ford

had expected to sell even half that many. And so, GM capitulated. In August 1964, work commenced at Chevrolet on a rival pony car, to be introduced in two years as a 1967 model. The project was kept a closely guarded secret, for rumors of the new car's development could only have further damaged the Corvair's already dismal sales pace.

In fact, in October 1964, with work on the new model proceeding apace, Bill Mitchell, GM's styling vice president — addressing a gathering of some of the corporation's junior engineers — was asked when General Motors would have an answer to the Mustang. Mitchell, knowing full well what was under development, deadpanned, "We *have* an answer to the Mustang. It's called Corvair!"

It was September 29, 1966, when the first Camaros appeared in Chevrolet showrooms across the country. Just as the Mustang had been derived from the Falcon, the Camaro borrowed liberally from the Chevy II. Only in this case it was a parallel development with the 1968 Nova, a much improved version of the little Chevy, not due for public display for another year.

The Camaro's concept was essentially the same as that of the Mustang: a sporty coupe with two-plus-two seating. Both cars featured long hood, short deck styling, but while the lines of the Mustang were clean and crisp, those of the Camaro were smooth and suggestively curvaceous.

There were other differences. The Mustang, like the Falcon, featured fully unitized body-and-frame construction. The first-generation (1962-1967) Chevy II's were built the same way. The result was a very solid little car, but one with a rather harsh ride and an unpleasantly high level of interior noise.

Chevrolet, in developing both the 1967 Camaro and the 1968 Nova, handled the problem by the relatively simple expedient of carrying the engine and front suspension on a bolt-on subframe, carefully insulated from the main body-and-frame section through the use of rubber cushions.

The popular American theme in those days seemed to be "Bigger is better." Accordingly, Chevrolet planned the Camaro to be three inches longer, four-and-a-quarter inches wider and 300 to 375 pounds heavier (depending upon body style) than the original Mustang. To cope with the extra weight the Camaro's base six-cylinder engine, at 230 cubic inches, was 15 percent larger than that of the Mustang.

Of course, Ford wasn't about to be caught napping. The question, however, was a familiar one: what to do for an encore? 121,538 Mustangs had been built during the abbreviated 1964 model run, followed by 559,451 for 1965 and 607,568 during the 1966 season — an astonishing total by anyone's standards. Nobody likes to mess around with a winning formula, obviously. And yet the demands of the marketplace — particularly with competition from Chevrolet looming on the horizon, and a redesigned Plymouth Barracuda as well — dictated that a new Mustang must appear.

Ford design executive Don Kopka described the challenge: "Our mission was to refine and improve the breed without losing any of the Mustang's personality

and without any sheet metal changes that would destroy the strong identity established by the million and a half Mustangs that were expected to be on the road before the 1967 model first saw the light of day."

Some assignment! But Ford's handling of the problem can only be termed "inspired." The styling theme of the original Mustang was preserved, yet the car — which had grown longer by two inches, wider by nearly three and heavier by just over a hundred pounds — managed to look hairier, yet softer and more rounded than its predecessor.

The result was an automobile that was changed, and yet somehow the same. A larger grille and rear panel, together with a deeper side scallop, gave it a stronger appearance. Fenders were a bit fuller, yet it would never have been mistaken for anything but a Mustang! The tread was widened, in order to provide space for the big-block 390-c.i.d. engine. This, too, contributed to the 1967 Mustang's beefier look — and to improved handling response, as well. This is not to suggest that the 390 itself had a felicitous effect upon the Mustang's handling. Capable of zero-to-sixty in seven seconds, a Mustang so-

equipped was a formidable machine on the drag strip, but the big engine created a substantial front-end weight bias. For that reason, a Mustang powered by the 271 horsepower version of the lightweight 289-c.i.d. block, and fitted with the optional handling package, was preferable by far as a *gran turismo* vehicle.

There were other modifications to the Mustang for 1967. The back seat was moved slightly rearward, in the interest of creating a tad more knee room in the rear compartment. Overall height was increased by half an inch, adding that much to the head room. Seats, interior trim and the instrument panel were all attractively redesigned and the trunk was a bit more commodious, though it was still pretty small.

Of greater significance were certain engineering changes. Rubber bushings at suspension attachment points reduced both noise and vibration. The front suspension was reworked to decrease the Mustang's tendency to understeer, though that characteristic remained noticeable. Polyethylene-filled ball-joint sockets helped to reduce steering effort and provided increased precision, while the turning circle was reduced by nearly five feet. And a new dual hydraulic braking system was an important safety factor.

It was to be expected that Chevy's Camaro — not to mention Plymouth's handsome new Barracuda, Pontiac's nimble Firebird, AMC's strikingly attractive Javelin and Lincoln-Mercury Division's in-house competitor, the Cougar — would cut sharply into the Mustang's 1967 sales. And this did indeed prove to be the case, although the Mustang managed very handily to outsell every one of its Johnny-come-lately rivals.

But certainly the Camaro was — as Dan Gurney put it, in a masterpiece of understatement — "a worthy competitor." Its front suspension, shared with

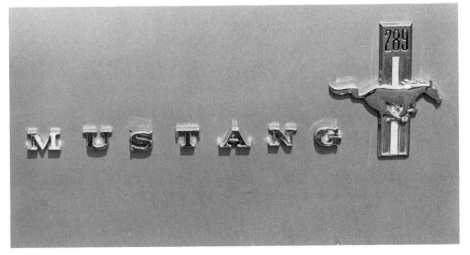

Right and below: '67 Mustang was going through that marque's first styling update since mid-'64 intro, while Camaro had just been brought to market in that model year, so styling was all-new. *Below right and bottom:* Camaro's slotted wheels look more businesslike than Mustang's attractive wire wheel covers.

SIA comparisonReport

Chevelle and the other GM A-bodied cars, was new, and while it was conventional enough, it was clearly *right!* The rear suspension borrowed the Chevy II's monoleaf springs, though they were shortened considerably for this application and came with different spring rates. There were problems with the single-leaf springs: some "judder" at high speeds, and a tendency to bottom-out under load. In time they were replaced by the more conventional multiple-leaf type. Nevertheless, in combination with the independent front suspension — in which the coil springs were located between the control arms instead of above them — they provided the Camaro with a surprisingly comfortable ride. And of course, by carrying the engine and front suspension on a carefully insulated sub-frame, noise and vibration were minimized.

From the start, Ford had offered a wide choice of powerplants for the Mustang, ranging from the anemic 170-c.i.d. Falcon six (replaced for 1965 by the more competent 200-c.i.d. version) to the lusty 271 horsepower, 289-c.i.d. V-8. The big 390 made its initial appearance for 1967. Chevrolet then went Ford one better, or rather *two* better, offering the Camaro buyer a choice of eight engines,

compared to six for the Mustang. There were two sixes and six V-8s in the Camaro catalog, ranging in horsepower from a mild but adequate 140 to a rousing 375 — 20 more, even, than Ford's 427, an engine available only in the limited production GT-500.

Both Camaro and Mustang came with a three-speed manual transmission as standard equipment, with different ratios furnished according to the engine selected. Both offered a four-speed manual or an automatic gearbox

at extra cost — again with ratios tailored to the specific application. The Camaro supplied the three-speed Turbo-Hydramatic only with the 325 horsepower 396 engine; otherwise the buyer, if he preferred shiftless driving, had to settle for the much less desirable Powerglide. Both cars were offered in either hardtop or convertible guise, and the Mustang was available in fastback configuration as well.

An interesting point of comparison is the fact that, while the 1967 Camaro hardtop outweighed its Mustang counterpart by just 160 pounds, in convertible form the margin was increased to 255 pounds. The difference is easily explained. Given the less rigid construction resulting from the Camaro's forward sub-frame, its convertible model — unlike the Mustang's — was subject to a good deal of torsional shake. Chevrolet remedied the situation by installing harmonic dampers — known in-house as "cocktail shakers" — at all four corners of the car. They were highly effective, but they did add weight!

The automotive press, already favorably inclined toward the Mustang, greeted the the Camaro with enthusiasm. Even the British, usually jaundiced in their view of American equipage, had kind words. "All told," said a *Motor Sport* writer, "the Camaro is the best sports-type car from across the Atlantic I have yet experienced."

Left: Camaro uses large single lens tail-lamps while Mustang, below, uses three vertical lenses per side.

Another British writer made some interesting comparisons between the Camaro and the Mustang. "Of the two cars, the Mustang feels as though it has the edge on torsional stiffness...but on the other hand the suspension on the Camaro is so superior that the Chevrolet ends up with a definite advantage.... The Mustang has softer, more comfortable seats.... It was, however, noisier in respect of engine and gear train sound.... Camaros were visibly better through the turns, and this was our opinion in everyday use. The Mustang has more practical styling and better static comfort, but the Camaro is more 'roadable,' especially at speed, and quieter."

We agree, up to a point. We give a clear edge to the Camaro when it comes to riding comfort and quiet operation, and we agree that the Mustang's seats are superior. We part company with our learned British colleague in assessing handling qualities, however. There, the little Ford with its more rigid construction, seems to us to enjoy the advantage.

Seats are very low in both cars, obviously a concession to styling; and lateral support is limited. The Mustang's cushions are deeper, however, and for a tall person its driving position is markedly superior to that of the Camaro. In the latter car we found the wheel literally resting on our long legs, a problem totally absent from the Mustang.

The gorgeous Camaro used by Vince Manocchi as his photo subject is so loaded with dealer-installed performance equipment that according to its owner, Bob Brannan, of Fullerton, California, its 327-c.i.d. engine churns out a blazing 300 horsepower! Bob tells us that this car, which is equipped with the Powerglide transmission, has been clocked at 140 miles an hour! Brannan, a member of the Crossroads Camaro Club, bought this car ten years ago for an incredible $200. Mechanically it was sound enough at the time, but Bob has had to refurbish it cosmetically.

Come to think of it, you may have seen this car before. For according to its owner, it appeared with Darrin McGavin in the motion picture *Night Stalker*. It was painted light blue at that time, but in the process of restoring it, Bob returned the car to its original Ermine White and Tuxedo Black color scheme. Driven sparingly now, the Camaro is a prized possession, one that has brought its owner a number of show trophies.

1967 Camaro Engines

	Bore/stroke	Displacement	Hp/rpm	Torque/rpm	Compression ratio
Base 6 cylinder	3.88/3.25	230.6	140/4,400	220/1,600	8.50:1
Optional 6 cylinder	3.88/3.53	249.8	155/4,200	235/1,600	8.50:1
Base V-8	4.00/3.25	326.7	210/4,600	320/2,400	8.75:1
Optional V-8	4.00/3.25	326.7	275/4,800	355/3,200	10.0:1
Optional V-8	4.00/3.01	302.4	290/5,800	290/4,200	11.0:1
Optional V-8	4.00/3.48	349.8	295/4,800	380/3,200	10.25:1
Optional V-8	4.09/3.76	395.2	325/4,800	410/3,200	10.25:1
Optional V-8	4.09/3.76	395.2	375/5,600	415/3,600	11.0:1

1967 Mustang Engines

	Bore/stroke	Displacement	Hp/rpm	Torque/rpm	Compression ratio
Base 6 cylinder	3.68/3.13	200.2	120/4,400	190/2,400	9.20:1
Base V-8	4.01/2.87	289.9	200/4,400	282/2,400	9.30:1
Optional V-8	4.01/2.87	289.9	225/4,800	305/3,200	9.30:1
Optional V-8	4.01/2.87	289.9	271/6,000	312/3,400	10.0:1
Optional V-9	4.05/3.78	389.6	320/4,800	427/3,200	10.5:1
Optional V-8*	4.13/3.98	426.5	355/5,400	462/2,800	10.5:1
*GT-500					

*Above and above right: comparisonReport Mustang uses base 200 horse 289 V-8, while Camaro uses high performance 300 horse 327 small block for go power. **Right and far right:** Camaro Rally Sport grille with its hidden headlamps gives car a meaner appearance than the deeply recessed Mustang grille and headlamps.*

1967 Camaro and Mustang Prices*

	Camaro	Mustang
Hardtop, 6-cylinder	$2,466	$2,461
Hardtop, V-8	$2,571	$2,567
Fastback, 6-cylinder		$2,592
Fastback, V-8		$2,698
Convertible, 6-cylinder	$2,704	$2,698
Convertible, V-8	$2,809	$2,804
*Prices shown are f.o.b. factory with standard equipment, federal excise tax included.		

SIA comparisonReport

Seeking a more modestly powered Camaro from which to record our driving impressions, we called on *SIA's* founder and first editor, Mike Lamm. Mike, of Stockton, California, bought his 1967 Camaro in 1969 from its original owner. He has added well over 100,000 miles to the 25,000 that appeared on the odometer at that time.

Lamm's Camaro is powered by the base, 210-horsepower, 327-c.i.d. V-8. Originally it was fitted with the two-speed Powerglide automatic transmission, a durable but somewhat inflexible unit. Mike replaced the slushbox some years ago with a Muncie four-speed — the same kind that would have been available as factory equipment in 1967. While he was about it, he improved the Camaro's handling characteristics by replacing the original suspension components with heavy duty springs and

shocks — air shocks being employed at the rear. The result, of course, was a substantial improvement in handling, together with a reduced tendency to roll in the turns.

Perhaps the most important modification made to this Camaro by its owner had to do with the brakes. Faced with a panic stop from a speed of 80 miles an hour someyears ago, Mike found that before that one stop was completed the brakes had turned to mush! A serious accident was narrowly averted. Disc/drum brakes had been a Camaro option from the beginning, but Lamm's car was fitted with the standard 9½-inch drums. Following the near-mishap, however, the optional brakes — together with rally wheels — were promptly installed.

To date the engine in Mike Lamm's Camaro has never been opened. At 130,000 miles it performs flawlessly and quietly. The car is nimble, quick, fun to drive; Mike describes it as "a great long-distance car." Shifts, with the Muncie four-speed, are crisp and precise, and

third gear is nice and tall. And if the handling isn't quite up to the standard of a comparably equipped Mustang, it's still far better than the average American automobile. We can easily understand why Mike hangs onto this car, now approaching its nineteenth birthday.

Our comparisonReport Mustang, on the other hand, had a more checkered early career, having been shamefully neglected when Tom Howard's parents took it over in 1975. The oil was as black as tar, and a number of crankcase changes were required over a period of several weeks before it was able to retain a normal coloration. The Cruise-O-Matic transmission was so badly shot that the car would barely move. There was a hole in the top, the interior appeared to have hosted a nest of mice, the paint was worn and faded and three of the wheel covers were missing.

But on the other hand, the body was straight and solid. Even the engine, once it was cleaned up and properly tuned, performed so well that in 1977 — having first rebuilt the transmission — the Howards took the Mustang on a trip from their Riverside, California, home to Detroit and return. The journey was made without incident as far as the automobile was concerned, but the tires were another matter entirely. A new set of radials had been fitted before the trip commenced. It happened, however, that this was at a time when one of the major rubber companies was experiencing no end of trouble with its radial tires, and before the Howards got back to River-

Specifications: 1967 Ford Mustang and 1967 Chevrolet Camaro

	1967 Ford Mustang	1967 Chevrolet Camaro
Price	$2,814 (f.o.b. factory, with standard equipment and base V-8 engine. Federal excise tax included.)	$2,809 f.o.b. factory, with standard equipment (federal excise tax included).
Standard equipment (partial list)	Heater/defroster, 2-speed electric windshield wipers with washer, front bucket seats, color-keyed carpeting front and rear, automatic courtesy lighting, backup lights, outside rearview mirror.	
Engine	90-degree V-8, cast en bloc	90-degree V-8, cast en bloc
Bore and stroke	4.01 inches x 2.87 inches	4 inches x 3¼ inches
Displacement	289.9 cubic inches	326.7 cubic inches
Maximum bhp @ rpm	200 @ 4,400	300 @ 5,000, photo subject car; 210 @ 4,600, test drive car
Maximum torque @ rpm	282 @ 2,400	360 @ 5,500, photo subject car; 320 @ 2,400, test drive car
Taxable horsepower	51.2	51.2
Compression ratio	9.3:1	10.5:1, photo subject car; 8.75:1, test drive car
Valve configuration	Ohv	Ohv
Valve lifters	Hydraulic	Solid, photo subject car; hydraulic, test drive car
Main bearings	5	5
Induction system	1-2 bbl Autolite carburetor, mechanical pump	1-4 bbl carb, photo subject car; 1-2 bbl carb, test drive car
Lubrication system	Pressure	Pressure
Exhaust system	Single	Dual, photo subject car; single, test drive car
Electrical system	12-volt	12-volt
Transmission	Cruise-O-Matic 3-speed automatic planetary gearset with torque converter	Powerglide automatic*, photo subject car; Muncie 4-speed, test drive car
Clutch		Single dry plate, test drive car
Diameter		10.4 inches, test drive car
Actuation		Mechanical, foot pedal (test drive car)
Differential	Hypoid	Hypoid
Ratio	2.79:1	3.08:1
Drive axles	Semi-floating	Semi-floating
Steering	Recirculating ball, power-assisted	Recirculating ball, power-assisted
Turns, lock-to-lock	3¾	3.0
Ratios, gear Ratio, overall	16.0:1 20.3:1	17.5:1 17.5:1
Turn circle (curb/curb)	37 feet, 2 inches	37 feet, 5 inches
Brakes	4-wheel hydraulic, drum type	Front disc, rear drum (power assisted on test-drive car)
Drum diameter	10 inches	Front rotors, 11 inches; rear drums, 9½ inches
Total swept area	251.3 square inches	332.4 square inches
Frame and body construction	All steel, unitized	Combination body-frame integral, with separate forward portion ladder frame
Body style	Convertible coupe	Convertible coupe
Suspension, front Suspension, rear	Independent, ball joints and coil springs Conventional, longitudinal 4-leaf springs	Independent with ball joints and coil springs Conventional, longitudinal mono-leaf springs
Tires	6.95/14	7.35/14
Wheels	Steel disc	Pressed steel
Wheelbase	108 inches	108.1 inches
Overall length	183.6 inches	184.7 inches
Overall width	70.9 inches	72.5 inches
Overall height	51.6 inches	51.4 inches
Front tread	58.1 inches	59 inches
Rear tread	58.1 inches	58.9 inches
Ground clearance	7½ inches	5 inches
Shipping weight	2,975 pounds	3,200 pounds
Capacities, crankcase	4 quarts (less filter)	4 quarts (less filter)
Automatic transmission	17 pints	6 pints
Cooling system	15 quarts (with heater)	17 quarts (with heater)
Fuel tank	16 gallons	18 gallons
Calculated data: Hp/c.i.d.	.692	.643, test drive car
Pounds/hp	14.9	15.2
Pounds/c.i.d.	10.3	9.79
Acceleration (from a *Motor Trend* road test)*	0-60: 9.5 seconds; ¼-mile: 17.0 seconds (81 mph). *Opt. 225 hp engine, automatic transmission	
Road tests (*Motor Trend*, December 1966, using same power train and brakes as *SIA*'s test drive car)		0-60: 10.7 seconds; ¼ mile: 18.2 seconds (77 mph); braking, from 60 mph; 151 feet
Braking (*Motor Trend* test, May 1967)	From 60 mph: 163 feet	
Model year production: Hardtop Fastback Convertible Total	356,271 71,042 44,808 472,121	195,776 25,141 220,917

SIA comparisonReport

side, three of the new skins had blown out.

The senior Howards added another 36,000 miles to the 80,000 already on the Mustang before they turned it over to their son Tom. Nearly nine years had passed since they rescued the forlorn little ragtop, and once again a fresh coat of paint was in order. A friend, John Loper, of Fayetteville, Arkansas, happened to be visiting Tom at just the appropriate time, and he refinished the Mustang in Brittany Blue metallic. Ken Carter, of Vancouver, British Columbia, fitted a new top to the car, and Tom rebuilt the engine.

Like the Camaro, the Mustang positions the driver very low. Leg room is better than the little Chevy, and the seats are more comfortable — though like the Camaro's they provide little lateral support. The steering wheel is positioned more vertically than most, a nice feature once one becomes accustomed to it. For a tall person, at least, the driving position is distinctly preferable to that of the Camaro.

Acceleration is good, especially for a car equipped with the base (200 horsepower) engine and an automatic transmission. There's that typical Mustang understeer, but it's not all that pronounced. On the whole we like the way this automobile handles. It corners relatively flat, it goes where it is pointed, the automatic transmission operates smoothly and the brakes — drums all

around, in this case — seem to do their job well. (We didn't try a panic stop from 80 miles an hour, however!) We even found that the Mustang, though it is very nimble, actually feels heavier than it really is. And if the ride betrays a little more harshness than that of the Camaro, it's still quite acceptable.

To summarize, then:
- The Camaro is distinctly the quieter of the two cars, though the difference is much less pronounced in the convertible than it would be in a hardtop.
- But the Mustang enjoys the advantage in handling.
- The Camaro provides a somewhat gentler ride.
- But the Mustang's seating is definitely the better of the two.
- For automatic transmission buyers, Ford's Cruise-O-Matic is an easy choice over Chevy's Powerglide.
- Stripped of all the extras, the Camaro seems somehow more barren than the Mustang.
- And the Camaro's mono-leaf rear suspension leaves a good deal to be desired.
- Standard brakes appear to be somewhat better on the Mustang.
- If you're getting into rough terrain, the Mustang's extra two-and-a-half inches of ground clearance would come in handy.
- And finally, there's the matter of styling. To each his own, of course. But from Day One we've felt that the crisp lines of the 1964-68 Mustangs were almost classic — and certainly classy! The Camaro's coke-bottle shape is unquestionably the sexier of the two, but.... □

Acknowledgements and Bibliography
Automotive Industries, *March 15, 1967; R.M. Clarke (editor),* Camaro, 1966-1970; *John Ethridge, "Mustang,"* Motor Trend, *December 1966; John Ethridge and Steven Kelly, "Trend-Setting Trio,"* Motor Trend, *October 1966;* Ford *factory literature; John Gunnell (editor),* Standard Catalog of American Cars, 1946-1975; *Dan Gurney, "Gurney Tests Chevy's Hot New Camaro,"* Popular Mechanics, *November 1966; Steven Kelly, "Camaro,"* Motor Trend,

Facing page, top row: "Thinwall" 289 V-8 was light in weight compared to the more traditionally cast Chevy V-8. Second row: Neither car has overly large or well-padded rear seats. Bottom: Both Mustang, left, and Camaro use two-pod instrument panels. This page, left and below: Seating position is a bit lower in the Camaro. Bottom: From the rear they're both good looking cars.

December 1966; Michael Lamm, The Great Camaro; Richard M. Langworth, Encyclopedia of American Cars, 1940-1970; Richard M. Langworth and Jan P. Norbye, Chevrolet, 1911-1985; David L. Lewis, Mike McCarville and Lorin Sorensen, Ford, 1903 to 1984; Tom McCahill, "McCahill Tests Chevy's New Camaro," Mechanix Illustrated, November 1966; "Camaro SS 350," Car and Driver, November 1966; "Mustang, Barracuda and Camaro," Road and Track, March 1967; "Mustang, Camaro and Barracuda," Motor Trend, May 1967.
Our thanks to Ray Borges and Linda Huntsman, Wm. F. Harrah Foundation, Reno, Nevada; Ralph Dunwoodie, Sun Valley, Nevada. Special thanks to Bob Brannan, Fullerton, California; Tom Howard, Riverside, California; Mike Lamm, Stockton, California.

The Missing Link: Plymouth's Barracuda

We didn't road-test the Barracuda along with the Camaro and the Mustang, but we have enough familiarity with the sporty little Plymouth to make some comparisons:

• Like the Mustang, the Barracuda was re-bodied for 1967. But unlike the Mustang, few changes were made to the chassis.

• Again like the Mustang, three body styles were offered: hardtop coupe, convertible and fastback. But in this instance the fastback was the best-seller.

• In contrast to both the Camaro and the Mustang, the Barracuda used mechanical rather than hydraulic valve lifters. Still, the clatter was minimal — probably less noticeable, as one commentator has observed, than the Mustang's fan.

• The Barracuda's three-speed Torque-flite automatic transmission was clearly better than the Mustang's Cruise-O-Matic and vastly superior to the Camaro's Powerglide.

• In its fastback form the Barracuda was the only practical cargo-hauler in the group, and the coupe has the only decent trunk in the pony car class. But their styling departs from the smart long hood/short deck configuration featured by the competition and obviously favored by the public.

• The Barracuda's level of fit and finish was not quite up to the standard of either the Camaro or the Mustang, but its gas mileage was the best of the three.

• Alone among the pony cars, the Barracuda fastback provided enough space for two adults to ride in the back seat in reasonable comfort.

• Like the Camaro, the Barracuda was best ordered with the optional disc brakes — at least for those drivers who frequented the fast lane.

• Front torsion bars, unique to the Barracuda among the pony cars, provided flat cornering and generally superior handling characteristics. A certain harshness was evident in the ride, however.

• The second-generation Barracuda was a fine little automobile, certainly one worthy of consideration among the corral full of pony cars that were offered in 1967. But although production showed a 64 percent increase over the 1966 model year, from a sales standpoint the Barracuda simply wasn't in the swim with either Mustang or Camaro.

Too bad. It deserved better.

1968 SHELBY GT 500-KR

by Dave Emanuel
photos by the author

SUGAR Ray Leonard was one of the most talented pugilists to ever wrap his hands in a pair of boxing gloves. He was quick, agile and powerful. But in spite of his consummate skills, his recent comeback attempt failed. Were it not for his continuing activities in television commercials, he would be all but forgotten — for reasons related not to skills, but to heft. He simply wasn't in the right weight category to enjoy a lingering limelight. As welterweight champion, he had gotten on stage, but in a world that equates bigger with better, the spotlights are focused on heavyweights.

In the mid-sixties, Carroll Shelby was pitched vis-a-vis a similar predicament. With the 1962 debut of his renowned Cobra, he had carved his initials indelibly in the annals of sports car history. And in 1965 he signed his name again with the introduction of the GT 350 Shelby Mustang. In their original configurations, with power provided by small-block Ford V-8s, both the Cobra and Shelby Mustang had blasted their way into the automotive world like shots fired from a howitzer. But as Bob Dylan so aptly phrased it, "The times, they [were] a-changin' "; with the emergence of Detroit muscle, both cars lost a touch of the original performance edge that had caused owners of competitive marques to turn green with envy.

In early 1965, Shelby set the situation partially right by infusing the Cobra with more deadly venom — a NASCAR style 427-cubic-inch Ford V-8 rated conservatively at 425 horsepower. But the GT 350 Mustang remained in need of a more powerful kick. The 306-hp, Shelby-modified 289 remained as the GT 350's sole powerplant (except for a *very* limited number of supercharged models), while 425-hp Corvettes, 360-hp GTOs, 335-hp Mustangs, 375-hp Chevelles and Camaros had come to the fore.

Shelby didn't wait long to answer the fusillade. With the 1967 model year, the GT 350 was given a big brother — the GT 500. Had it been practicable to insert a member of Ford's FE engine family in the 1966 Mustang, the Shelby GT 500 would have undoubtedly appeared a year earlier. But it wasn't until Ford restyled the Mustang in 1967 that the engine compartment grew to sufficient girth to readily accept a 390, 427 or 428 powerplant. With a 390-cubic-inch Mustang available directly from Ford, Shelby selected the 428 to insure that the GT 500 would enjoy a performance advantage over its cousin from Dearborn.

From the choice of engines, it is clear that the GT 500 was intended to be more a civilized road car than a brutal race machine. Had the reverse been true, the 427, which had seen service in a variety of competition applications, would have been selected. The difference between the engines was considerably more than a single cubic inch. With its longer stroke (3.984 inches as opposed to 3.788 inches) the 428 was more proficient at producing low-speed and midrange torque, making the GT 500 a very docile automobile. Even with dual 600 CFM Holley four-barrel carburetors, 10.5:1 compression ratio and a hydraulic lifter cam that opened and closed the valves with great enthusiasm, the engine was extremely well mannered. It could be taken anywhere without embarrassing or angering its owner.

No doubt it was with tongue firmly implanted in cheek that Shelby personnel foisted a rating of 355 horsepower upon the public. According to Rick Kopec, author of the *Shelby American*

Guide, "...this engine probably put out close to 400 horsepower. But no one at Shelby American would ever admit to anything near that magic number." The conservative rating wasn't intended to hoodwink potential buyers but was aimed at their nemesis, the insurance carrier who used high-power ratings as an excuse to raise the premium ante.

Insurance cost wasn't the only potential problem created by the 428 engine. With its greatly increased torque output, changes in driveline configuration were essential. Whereas Ford's C-4 automatic transmission (optional on GT 350) was an ideal mate for the 289, the 428 required a heftier partner; coupling a circus fat lady with the Thin Man just wouldn't work. The heavy-duty C-6 Cruise-O-Matic was more what the matchmaker had in mind. Its counterpart for standard shift-it-yourself applications was Ford's "top-loader" close-ratio four-speed manual transmission.

Coupled with the optional automatic was a 3.25:1 ratio rear axle, while output from the four-speed was routed through a 3.50:1 ring and pinion assembly. Both ratios were somewhat higher than those used in the GT 350 (3.89 with a four-speed, 3.50 with automatic), reflecting the 428's increased torque capacity.

Engines and power trains weren't the only distinctive aspects of the 1967 Shelby GTs. It would have been terribly

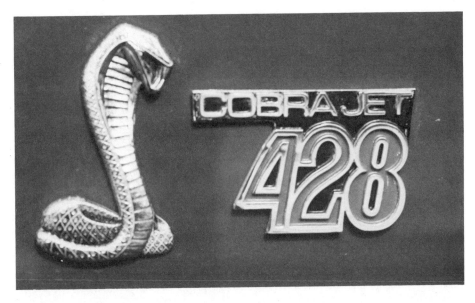

gauche of Shelby and company (not to mention completely out of character) to have produced a vehicle that could be easily mistaken for a proletarian Mustang; hence the GTs achieved distinction by virtue of extensively restyled front and rear body panels. A fiberglass hood with a split scoop and a redesigned grille opening provided the car with a unique nose which was complemented by a tail customized with a spoiler molded into the deck lid and upper fender extensions. Two air scoops posi-

tioned high and low on the rear quarter, special taillights, high beams mounted in the center of the grille and side stripes completed the restyling package.

The suspension also benefited from the Shelby touch. But then it had to — the GT 500 outweighed its 289-engined baby brother by some 500 pounds (perhaps that's the origin of the GT 500 nomenclature), most of which was attributable to the ponderous mass of cast iron residing in the engine compartment. Since an integral part of the

THE KR MEANS "KING OF THE ROAD"

1968 SHELBY

Shelby Mustang character was aggressive road manners and superior handling capability, the cars had since their inception been treated to revised suspensions. But with the GT 500's frame-warping front end bulk, suspension rework was absolutely essential merely to imbue the car with maneuverability superior to that of a delivery truck.

As evidenced by contemporary road tests, the Shelby American crew did a commendable job in neutralizing the effects of the Big Bertha engine. According to *Road and Track*, "As for handling, the GT 500 is something less than we've come to expect from Shelby's cars but still very good in comparison to the typical American sedan. On the other hand, considering the weight distribution, it's better than we would have thought possible only a couple of years ago. With 58 percent of its total weight on the front wheels, we'd expect it to have understeer akin to that of the USS United States, but it doesn't. As we said, it goes where it's pointed." In a test evaluating both the GT 350 and 500, *Sports Car Graphic* offered a concurring appraisal. "In corners, the 500 demands a considerably tighter 'hand on the reins,' but it gets around surprisingly well, with less understeer than we expected."

Although 1967 had been a high water mark in terms of sales, it was essentially a year of transition. Whereas the first Shelby Mustangs were basic, finely tuned, high-performance sports cars, in the GT 500, the sports car blood lines had begun to fade. Yet in its first year of production, this model outsold the GT 350 by a margin of almost two-to-one; the buying public was clearly more captivated by the luxury/GT package than

Driving Impressions

The French have a term for it. *Deja vu.* Literally translated — as literally that is, as French can be rendered into English — it means "already seen," but as generally employed, the term describes a haunting sensation that invades the cerebrum when you experience something for the first time, but feel as though you've been through it before.

That's precisely what I experienced when I climbed behind the wheel of Rick Galtelli's 1968 Shelby GT 500-KR. I'd never been in the car before, nor had I ever previously driven a Shelby, but it all felt so familiar — the automatic transmission's "T"-handle shifter, a large speedometer and tach set into a wood-grain dash panel, the warbling sound of the exhaust, a steering wheel that seemed to be positioned too high.

Unquestionably, I felt as though I had been in the car previously because I had, over the years, driven a number of plain vanilla Mustangs with big-block engines stuffed beneath their bonnets. And while much has been written about the effect of the alterations wrought upon the Mustang chassis by Carroll Shelby and company, the GT 500-KR has that unmistakable feel of a proletarian Mustang with "the big engine"; it derives from a weight distribution that has nearly 60 percent of the vehicle's mass weight teetering over its front wheels.

The impression that is communicated through the steering wheel is, to say the least, unsettling; the car appears to have a mind of its own. In no uncertain terms, it tells you, "We will either drive straight ahead or make nice easy turns. Try pushing me around a corner and I'll show you what plowing fields is all about. Is that understood?" One feels compelled to bow (a very difficult maneuver when you're in the driver's seat) and reply, "Yes your eminence" (or is it imminence — as in danger?) and remain an obedient servant to the machine.

In actual fact, the KR's bark is worse than its bite. Negotiating a turn at higher than prudent speeds, understeer — buckets of it — is unquestionably in evidence, yet in spite of the disquieting sensation that the car is about to make an off-road foray, it is surprisingly adept at keeping all four tires on the macadam. The car remains relatively flat and stable while being taken through a corner, and logic dictates that consternation is unjustified. But logic be damned, the gut-tightening feeling that the ponderous mass up front is about to pull you into the weeds is ever-present.

Part of the problem owes to the steering gear. Although the ratio is listed at 16:1, roughly the same as a late model Corvette, response is painfully slow. It feels almost as if the steering wheel is communicating with the front wheels through an obtuse translator. A degree of precision and control is lost in the process.

While the hulking 427 engine does compromise lateral alacrity, it works wonders with straight-line performance. It requires but one stab at the accelerator to determine that Ford Motor Company was indeed playing charades when it rated the Cobra-Jet engine at 335 horsepower. With a curb weight in excess of 3,500 pounds, the GT 500 is not a light car, but it accelerates as if it were. Contemporary road tests cited 0-60 times of 6.0-6.8 seconds and quarter mile clockings of 14 seconds flat or less. Those figures were achieved amidst an abundance of performance compromising wheelspin, so the journalistic claims that the engine was producing close to 400 horsepower appear to be quite accurate.

The engine is clearly of the Muscle Car idiom — power without temperamental problems. The hydraulic lifter camshaft is sufficiently demure that the engine starts easily, idles smoothly and runs quietly. Fully depressing the accelerator pedal will bring a roar from the engine compartment as the Holley carburetor opens all four barrels to the onrushing air, but that aside, the Cobra-Jet engine displays manners that would even make Emily Post proud.

One of the reasons that both engine and road noise are not obtrusive is that the KR, like all 1968 GT 350s and GT 500s, was constructed at Ford's Metuchen, New Jersey, plant and shipped to the A.O. Smith Company of Ionia, Michigan, where the Shelby treatment was administered. Previously, semi-completed bodies were shipped from Ford's San Jose, California, or Metuchen plants to the Shelby American facilities in Southern California. But at the end of 1967,

Shelby's lease on his manufacturing facilities, a couple of hangars at Los Angeles International Airport, expired, necessitating a new arrangement. It certainly would have been possible to open a new plant in California, but it was more practical to contract with Smith, which had expertise not only in vehicle assembly, but in the manufacture of fiberglass parts.

The Shelby crew might have been more "creative," but Smith, having been a supplier to several auto companies, had a better handle on assembly-line production techniques. The later Shelbys undoubtedly lack some of the "character" that earmarked earlier models, but they also seem to be bereft of the squeaks and rattles that plague the 1965-1967 cars.

I've never been particularly keen on Ford products, yet I was saddened in 1970 when I learned that there would be no more Shelby GTs. They were a refreshing splash of individuality in a desert of mass-produced sameness. But after driving Galtelli's "King of the Road" GT 500, I came to understand why Carroll Shelby brought the curtain down. The federal government was encroaching more and more on the automakers' domain, and that was bringing an end to the days of true individuality.

While the GT 500-KR has its faults, it is certainly an enjoyable car to drive. But it lacks the unique personality that characterized the original Shelby GTs. Aside from cosmetics, the splash of individuality has vanished. The same federal safety and emissions standards that caused a cessation of Cobra and in a sense GT 350 production (the model designation was continued, but with the 1968 switch to a standard 302 engine, sports car performance had departed), dictated that the KR be little more than a gussied-up version of a production Mustang — a Cobra-Jet with stripes and a few fiberglass body panels. Consequently, Shelby American was no longer able to manufacture sports cars; it had been forced into the business of producing luxury/GT vehicles that were cut from the same mold as those being sold by Ford, General Motors and Chrysler. What was the point of continuing?

specifications

Illustrations by Russell von Sauers, The Graphic Automobile Studio

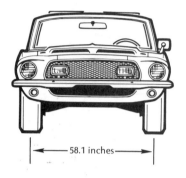

← 58.1 inches →

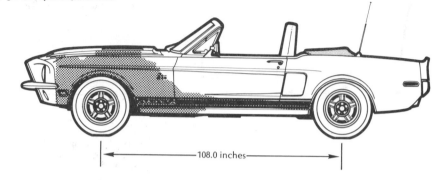

← 108.0 inches →

1968 Shelby GT 500-KR

Price	$4,594. As equipped, $4,963.
Optional equipment	Power steering, power brakes, automatic transmission, tilt wheel, AM radio, limited slip rear axle, 428 engine, heater and defroster, competition handling package, center console, deluxe interior, heavy duty cooling system and integral roll bar all included with GT 500-KR package

ENGINE

Type	V-8 ohv
Bore & stroke	4.13 inches x 3.984 inches
Displacement	428 cubic inches
Horsepower	335 at 5,200 rpm
Torque	440 at 3,400 rpm
Compression ratio	10.6:1
Induction system	Holley 715 CFM 4-bbl on "high volume" intake manifold
Exhaust system	Dual, 2.25-inch diameter
Electrical system	12-volt battery/coil

TRANSMISSION

Type	3-speed automatic
Ratios: 1st	2.46:1
2nd	1.46:1
3rd	1:1
Reverse	2.20:1

DIFFERENTIAL

Type	Hypoid semi-floating, limited slip
Ratio	3.50:1

STEERING

Type	Semi-reversible, recirculating ball, power assisted
Ratio	16.1:1
Turns lock to lock	3.7
Turning circle	37.16 feet

BRAKES

Type	Hydraulic with vacuum power assist, 11.3-inch diameter ventilated front discs, 10.0-inch x 1.75-inch rear drums
Total swept area	282.5 square in.

CHASSIS & BODY

Construction	Unit steel body welded to reinforced platform chassis
Body	2-door convertible with integral roll bar

SUSPENSION

Front	Independent SLA, coil springs, double-acting tubular shocks, .94-inch anti-sway bar
Rear	Live axle with 4-leaf semi-elliptic springs, double-acting adjustomatic tubular shocks, anti-sway bar
Wheels	15-inch x 7-inch cast aluminum alloy
Tires	F60 x 15-inch Goodyear Polyglass

WEIGHTS AND MEASURES

Wheelbase	108.0 inches
Overall length	186.81 inches
Overall height	51.8 inches
Overall width	70.9 inches
Front tread	58.1 inches
Rear tread	58.1 inches
Curb weight	3,695 pounds

PERFORMANCE

Maximum speed	132 mph
Acceleration: 0-60	6.7 seconds
Standing start ¼-mile	13.7 seconds and 104 mph
Fuel economy	10-14 mpg. Premium required

Below: I.d. on horn bar. Top center: 428 engine pumps out 440 pounds of torque. Below center: Ram Air induction system included special manifolding. Right: Fiberglass hood uses large, functional row of louvers on each side.

1968 SHELBY

by the race car in street clothing. That attitude was reflected in the vehicles brought to market in 1968, the most effete machines yet to bear the Shelby nameplate. Where staccato exhaust notes, played by a long-duration mechanical lifter camshaft, had once pulsed from the tailpipes of the GT 350, the 1968 model mustered but a soft melody; the high-performance 289 engine had been replaced with a lackluster 302. And along with the increase in displacement, came a *decrease* of 56 horsepower.

The second incarnation of the GT 500 was mechanically identical to its predecessor save for the elimination of the sole piece of internal combustion exotica that graced the 1967 version — the dual four-barrel induction system. In softening the car for greater market potential, the dual carburetors had been supplanted by a single 715 CFM Holley four-barrel. Surprisingly, with the reduction in carburetion came an increase of five horsepower.

Other changes for 1968 included revisions to the hood, taillights, grille opening and identifying emblems. The cars were no longer simply Shelby GTs — they now had the word "Cobra" included in their official designation. The other news for the 1968 model year was the first appearance of a convertible in the Shelby line. Both the 350 and 500 were offered in drop-top configuration.

During 1967 and early 1968, Ford had been having great success in the drag-racing arena. Seeking to capitalize on the sales potential generated by performance in sanctioned competition, Ford introduced a new engine — the Cobra Jet 427 — as a mid-year option. The new powerplant melded the existing block and reciprocating assembly with large-port cylinder heads and intake manifold taken from the 427. And once again, the tongue-in-cheek horsepower raters sharpened their pencils. The Cobra Jet engine was alleged to produce only 335 horsepower — in spite of the fact that torque had been increased by 20 lbs./ft.

Rather than simply substituting the

new engine for the old, and maintaining a business-as-usual posture, Shelby developed a new model around it. Thus the GT 500-KR or "King of the Road" was born — amidst a splash of publicity, of course. Not that it wasn't warranted. Since the KR was replacing the standard GT 500, Shelby took some pains to upgrade the product line. Extra bracing was added to the shock towers to increase front structural rigidity; staggered rear shock absorbers were utilized on four-speed KRs to control wheel hop; engine oil coolers were included when air conditioning was ordered; wider rear brake shoes and drums and heavy-duty wheel cylinders were fitted to improve stopping capability. And on the outside, the identifying markings were revised with the addition of either "KR" or "Cobra Jet."

As in the previous year, Shelby Mustangs set a new sales record in 1968; total production tallied 4,450 vehicles, the highest number ever. But rather than being a portent of future success, 1968 marked a turning point. Events

outside Shelby American's sphere of influence, specifically escalating insurance rates and the increasing stringency of exhaust emission and safety regulations, brought new hardships to the manufacturers of specialty vehicles and those who purchased them. As a result, sales dropped to 3,150 units in 1969. Rather than push on through the 1970 model year, Shelby decided to quit while he was ahead. Once the decision was made, the cars in process — a total of 601 — were completed. And then came an event that only a few years before would have seemed unthinkable. Carroll Shelby hung up his guns and rode off into the sunset. □

Acknowledgements and Bibliography
Road and Track, *various issues, 1964-1968*; Sports Car Graphic, *various issues, 1967-1968*; The Shelby American, *by Richard J. Kopec;* Shelby Buyer's Guide, *by Richard J. Kopec.*
Our thanks to Brenda Holland and Bill Mosley. Special thanks to Rick Galtelli for making his car available.

1969 Mustang Grandé

Bargain-Basement 'Bird

by M. Park Hunter
photos by the author

FORD had a hit on its hands with the original Mustang, and it had a problem. How do you follow a car that sets a world record, selling 680,989 copies during the extended model year from April 1964 to August 1965? Even counting just 1965 production, Mustang would have ranked seventh in the industry as a car company, outrunning the entire output of veterans Dodge, Mercury, Rambler and others.

Dearborn came up with two answers. First, don't tamper with success. The 1966 Mustang was a near twin to the original, and the '67-'68 models changed only in detail. Production the second year was an astonishing 607,568, then fell to 472,121 in 1967 and 317,148 for 1968. Competition was part of the reason for the drop: Mercury got its Cougar and General Motors introduced the popular Camaro/Firebird twins in 1967.

Second, Ford began to treat the Mustang almost as if it were a separate division. Part of Mustang's appeal was that buyers could choose from a smorgasbord of options and literally build a car to taste. When the greatly revised 1969 version debuted, Ford bundled packages of trim, chassis and engine tuning together to create what amounted to several models of Mustang.

Plain-vanilla ponies came as hardtop coupes, fastbacks or convertibles. Three special models reflected the Mustang's strong performance following: the Mach I with its hood scoop was the street rodder's choice, while the mid-year Boss 302 and Boss 429 reflected Ford's Trans-Am and NASCAR efforts.

A fourth model, the Mustang Grandé, was offered as a coupe with luxury trim-

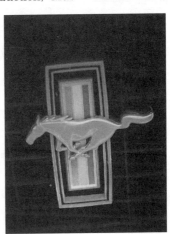

mings. Although drivetrain options included the fire-breathing big-blocks, Grandés came standard with the old-aunt 115-horsepower six and were most commonly equipped with the 302- or 351-cubic-inch V-8 and automatic transmission. Tuned for comfort over handling and decked out like a miniature parlor, the Grandé seemed an anomaly at the time and has been quickly forgotten by ponycar enthusiasts.

However, the Grandé was actually quite in line with the original concept for the Mustang. After Ford canned the two-place '55-'57 Thunderbird in favor of the bulkier, glitzier four-seat Squarebird of 1958, the company received numerous requests for a small, sporty T-Bird revival. Management also considered a radical mid-engine sports car before wisely choosing the middle ground that became the Mustang.

But the extremists in favor of all-out performance or upper-crust luxury weren't denied. Through the services of Carroll Shelby, some Mustangs were converted into rough-and-rude pure sports cars. And for 1969, the Grandé made the Mustang into a grand-touring personal luxury coupe very much in the style of the Thunderbird, but on a smaller scale.

Like Thunderbird, the Grandé's suspension was adjusted to sacrifice all-out performance in the interest of greater smoothness. Ford engineers really sweated the details, even installing voided rubber bushings in the front eyes of the rear spring mounts. These softer bushings allowed the axle to move back slightly over bumps, soaking up the impact and transmitting less noise to

Mustang styling was all-new for 1969 including quad headlamps and wider width and length, although the original pony's 108-inch wheelbase remained unchanged.

1969 Mustang

the chassis and interior. Axle movement is a no-no for serious performance nuts, but on the Grandé the trade-off was deemed acceptable.

Grandé shared a new body design with all 1969 Mustangs. The 108-inch wheelbase was retained from earlier models, but the new pony was four inches longer and a half-inch wider and shorter. Weight was up about 50 pounds across the board. The Mustang's independent front suspension and live rear axle changed little; the big differences were reserved for the styling.

Up front, all Mustangs shared new quad headlamps. Low beams tunnelled into the fenders, and new high beam

lamps were mounted in the corners of the protruding grille. Door glass no longer included a swing-out vent window. The traditional cove in the sheet-metal sides was eliminated. In its place, fastbacks mounted nostril-like intakes at the top of the rear fenders.

The Grandé coupe got rear-facing faux scoops lower on the rear fender. Other Grandé-specific styling touches included tastefully muted tape stripes along the tops of the fenders and doors, streamlined "racing-style" mirrors, chrome wheel well trim, wire hubcaps and vinyl roofs. Wheels mounted high-quality Goodyear Power Cushion bias-ply tires. The result was a surprisingly subdued and tasteful take on standard Mustang styling.

Inside, Ford stylists pulled out all the stops. Woodgraining was applied in huge swaths to the door panels and

twin-cove dashboard. The dash ahead of the passenger mounted a large clock and Grandé identification plate. Carpeting was rather plusher than normal, and underneath it engineers applied 55 extra pounds of sound-deadening material.

The seats were upholstered in a combination of vinyl and hopsack. *Car Life* testers described the hopsack material as a "country club burlap," appreciating its softness and grippy texture. Holding with Mustang tradition, comfortable front bucket seats were offset by thinly padded, cramped rear seats that squeezed like buckets but rode like benches.

In 1969, 71 percent of Mustang buyers chose the console-shifted automatic over the three- and four-speed manuals. Ford's competent Cruise-O-Matic was very much in keeping with the Grandé's character. Almost 82 percent of buyers picked a V-8 over the standard six, and for the majority of Grandé customers this meant a version of Ford's respected 302 and 351 family of engines.

These small-block engines dated back to the Fairlane motor introduced in 1962. Originally offered in 221- and 260-cubic-inch versions, this was the lightest cast-iron V-8 on the market and a fine performer, as demonstrated by the Shelby Cobras. The 289 variant arrived in 271-horsepower trim for 1963 and would be the top engine option for the Mustang's debut. In the quest for more power, Ford offered big-block 390 V-8s and the huge 427, 428, and 429 engines in later years. These gorillas exacerbated the Mustang's tendency to understeer, though, necessitating a number of engineering fixes to the front suspension.

For 1968, the old Fairlane engine was optionally stroked to 302 cubic inches, delivering 220 horsepower with a two-barrel carburetor. The following year the 289 was dropped and the 302 became the smallest V-8. Ordered as the Boss 302, this engine came in a hot Trans-Am tuned version good for 290 horsepower with a four-barrel carb. Meanwhile, another stroke job on the gutsy small block produced a 351-cubic inch V-8, available with 250 or 290 horsepower depending on carburetion.

The 302 and 351 engines were perfectly suited to the Grandé, providing smooth power proportional to the capabilities of the chassis. Dig was especially good at low rpms, just where it was needed for around-town traffic. At the same time, these weren't exactly high-winding sports car motors. *Car Life* said, "The 351 will turn 4,800 [rpm] in the lower gears, but when it arrives, it sounds like an office worker at the top of four flights of stairs."

Car Life's 1969 test of a 351-equipped Grandé produced 0-60 times of 8.0 seconds, respectable but not scorching. In

Above: *Headlamps were swept back radically compared to earlier Mustangs. High beams are in grille.* **Below:** *Fuel filler stayed in center of rear panel, as in previous years. Vinyl top was part of Grandé package as were,* **bottom,** *wire wheel covers.*

contrast, Mustangs with hotter motors were rocket ships. The editors squeezed 6.9 seconds out of a 1969 Boss 302 and a smoking 5.5-second launch from a Mach 1 with the 428 engine.

Yet *Car Life* was quite happy with the Grandé's performance. They noted it was faster than more mundane cars yet easier to drive and more fuel efficient than the hot ticket 'stangs. Best of all, the small-block engine didn't compromise the Mustang's handling. The magazine's road test was conducted in rainy weather, yet even in the wet the Grandé coped with ham-fisted techniques on curves and rewarded skilled drivers with poised cornering.

Editors also swooned over the car's optional front disc/rear drum brakes. Ford products in this era were building a reputation for above-average braking ability. Partly this was due to the generally abysmal state of brakes in the sixties, and partly it was because of Ford's policy of equipping all press fleet cars with discs even though only a third of customers ordered them in 1969. Mostly, it was because the brakes really were good: *Car Life* repeatedly hauled the Grandé from 80-0 mph at near-record rates without suffering significant fade.

Altogether, the Grandé was a nifty package combining the nimbleness of a Mustang with the luxurious refinement of the Thunderbird. Priced about $2,000 less than the 'Bird, it should have sold like hotcakes. Yet Ford's multi-model Mustang strategy didn't work. Production slipped again in 1969 to 300,682 and the Grandé managed only 22,182

illustrations by Russell von Sauers, The Graphic Automobile Studio

specifications

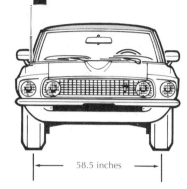

58.5 inches

108.0 inches

1969 Mustang Grandé

Base price	$2,950
Price as featured	$3,527

ENGINE

Type	"F"-code cast-iron ohv V-8
Bore x stroke	4.00 inches x 3.00 inches
Displacement	302 cubic inches
Compression ratio	9.5:1
Horsepower @ rpm	220 @ 4,600
Torque @ rpm	295 @ 2,400
Main bearings	5
Valve actuation	Hydraulic lifters, overhead rocker arms
Carburetor	Motorcraft 2-barrel

DRIVETRAIN

Transmission	Select-Shift Cruise-O-Matic
Type	3-speed automatic with torque converter
Shifter	Console mounted
Ratios: 1st	2.46:1, trans; 6.77:1, overall
2nd	1.46:1, trans; 4.02:1, overall
3rd	1.00:1, trans; 2.75:1, overall
Final drive ratio	2.75:1
Differential type	Hypoid
Shift point, 1st to 2nd	48.5 mph @ 4,400 rpm (w/351 engine)
Shift point, 2nd to 3rd	81.7 mph @ 4,400 rpm (w/351 engine)

STEERING

Type	Power linkage assist, recirculating ball gear
Turns lock-to-lock	3.74
Ratio	20.3:1
Turning circle	37.6 feet

BRAKES

Type	Front disc, 11.3-inch diameter, 2.07 inches, width; rear drum, 10.0-inch diameter, 20.0 inches, width
Actuation	Power-assisted hydraulic
Total swept area	339.5 square inches
Line pressure	795 p.s.i. at 100 lb. pedal

SUSPENSION

Frame type	Unitized
Front suspension	Short-long arm independent, drag strut, ball joints, coil springs, tube-type shock absorbers
Rear suspension	Hotchkiss live axle, semi-elliptical leaf springs, tube-type shock absorbers
Rim size	14x5JJ
Attachment pattern	5 bolts, 4.5-inch-diameter spread
Tire type	Goodyear Power Cushion
Tire size	E78-14
Inflation pressure (f/r)	24/24 p.s.i.

WEIGHTS AND MEASURES

Wheelbase	108 inches
Overall length	187.4 inches
Overall width	71.3 inches
Overall height	51.3 inches
Frontal area	20.3 sq. ft.
Front track	58.5 inches
Rear track	58.5 inches
Curb weight	3,125 pounds (w/351 engine)
Weight distribution	56.4/43.6 percent (w/351 engine)

Door opening width	43.0 inches
Head room (f/r)	37.4/35.8 inches (f/r)
Shoulder room (f/r)	56.0/54.7 inches (f/r)
Hip room (f/r)	20 inches x 2 seats/52.0 inches
Leg room (f/r)	39.0/27.0 inches
Trunk liftover height	33.0 inches
Luggage space	9.8 cubic feet

CAPACITIES

Number of passengers	4
Crankcase	5.0 quarts
Radiator	15.4 quarts
Fuel tank	20 gallons
Transmission	26.0 pints
Differential	4 pints

PERFORMANCE

Top speed	119.2 mph at 4,400 rpm
Acceleration: 0-30 mph	3.4 seconds (w/351 engine)
0-40 mph	4.7 seconds
0-50 mph	6.3 seconds
0-60 mph	8.0 seconds
0-70 mph	10.0 seconds
0-80 mph	12.6 seconds
0-90 mph	16.2 seconds
0-100 mph	21.6 seconds
Passing, 30-70 mph	6.6 seconds
Standing 1/4 mile	15.59 seconds/89.09 mph
Fuel consumption	12-15 mpg

(All performance data is from a February 1969 *Car Life* road test of a Mustang Grandé equipped with the 290-horsepower, 351-cubic-inch V-8 and automatic transmission. The 302-cubic-inch V-8 in our feature car would have somewhat slower performance and better fuel economy.)

Sources: *Car Life* road test (2/69)

Right: 1969 Mustangs looked huskier and indeed were slightly larger than earlier cars. *Facing page, top:* "Air inlets" of previous years became relocated "air outlets" on Grandé. Mirrors changed from chrome to body color. *Below:* Grandé interior was ultra plush, with high quality leatherette and hopsack seating and much more sound deadening than regular editions. *Bottom:* Not intended as a high-performance pony, Grandé's oomph with 302 is more than adequate. With 351 it really hauls.

1969 Mustang

copies, just over seven percent of the total.

Mustang sales continued to plummet the next few years while Ford introduced ever bulkier models. As emissions controls, fuel crunches and high insurance tariffs drained the life from truly muscular cars, Ford and other manufacturers turned to paint, stickers and the illusion of performance. Customers who couldn't get speed opted for comfort, ordering more luxury options each year. By 1973, nearly all Mustangs sold with power steering, three-quarters had power disc brakes, and over half were equipped with air-conditioning.

And thus a funny thing happened: As the hot engines and purebred sports models went away, the plush Grandé accounted for more of the pie each year. In 1973 almost 19 percent of Mustang sales came from the Grandé. Porcine Mustangs simply weren't the right cars for the new decade, but the Grandé was as good as they got.

Ford did better in 1974, dumping the whales in favor of a shrimp-sized Mustang II. It wasn't fast, but it handled reasonably well, got great fuel economy and was far swankier than the Pinto. In place of the Grandé, Ford offered luxury trimmings on the Mustang Ghia. Purists may whine that the Grandés were out of character for America's favorite performance machine, but by design or by accident they became what the market wanted.

Driving Impressions

Our featured 1969 Mustang Grandé belongs to Doug Miller of Indianapolis, Indiana. The clean little coupe has been in his family since new. Miller's grandmother used it during the summers and stored it while she wintered in Florida.

In 1981, Miller bought the car and drove it during his senior year of high school. Since then the Mustang has spent most of its time in storage. The odometer shows a hair over 40,000 miles.

Miller says, "I feel sorry for the car, actually. If it were in another family, somebody would be like, 'Oooo... I love this car!' We just haven't done anything with it. We're not big collectors and we don't take it to shows. Mostly, it just sits."

Not surprisingly, the Grandé is in superb, near-original condition. Aside from belts and hoses, the only significant deviation from stock is a set of

*Above: Combo of front discs/rear drums greatly improved Mustang's braking compared to pre-'69 cars. **Below:** Two round coves continue dash theme set in '67.*

1969 Mustang Grandé Resources

CLUBS

The Mustang Club of America Inc.
3588 Highway 138, Suite 365
Stockbridge GA 30281
770-477-1965
http://www.mustang.org
(5,000 members, monthly magazine, local regions, annual meets, $30/year)

Mustang Owners Club
2720 Tennessee NE
Albuquerque, NM 87110
505/296-2554
(500 members, bimonthly magazine, $15/year)

1969 Mustang

headers and dual exhausts Miller put on when he was in high school. At the time, it was the cool thing to do. The 220-horsepower, two-barrel 302 V-8 and automatic transmission are otherwise untouched.

"I did save the original exhaust manifolds in the basement of my parents' house all these years. Even then we knew it would be a collectible some day," Miller says. He adds sheepishly, "But just this past year my parents moved from the house they'd been in forever. I don't know whether they sold [the manifolds] in the sale or just threw them away, but now they're gone."

Most '69 Mustangs one sees these days are the steroid-enhanced performance models with their shaker hoods and gaping ducts. It's easy to forget how right the basic Mustang proportions are underneath all that hokum. Thus the Grandé's appearance is almost shockingly tasteful at first sight.

The formal vinyl roof, wire wheelcovers and thin chrome accents do the coupe body justice. Modest black-and-gold tape stripes along the top of the fenders and doors actually make the lime gold paint look good, something I never thought I'd say about this particular shade of green. The only jarring notes are the imitation vents on the flanks, which look like the tacked-on plastic blemishes they are. Probably Ford stylists felt obligated to put something here because the scalloped sides of the '65-'68 Mustangs had provided such a strong identity.

No matter what you've heard about the shoddy quality of American cars in the late sixties and seventies, this particular Grandé is surprisingly well built. The doors shut cleanly, the trunk lid is light and tight, and trim and body panels all line up. There aren't even any odd squeaks or rattles.

Our test drive takes place on a cold November day. Despite rarely receiving exercise, the 302 cranks for just a few seconds before firing up. The rather fast idle soon calms down and the engine proves to be beautifully tuned and smooth running. There's no stutter or hesitation, no lunging or surging in response to the throttle.

Under the whip, the Grandé's drivetrain produces easy power and alert shifts with no histrionics like smoking tires or howling exhaust notes. It's more of an executive express than an all-out hot rod. In the passenger compartment we hear only a velvety hum, like a late model Mustang 5.0 motor heard through a thick mattress. This isn't sur-

Above: 302 V-8 is rated at 220 horses. It offered a combo of strong performance and excellent fuel economy for its time. Below: Woodgrain trim on doors helps gussy up Grandé interior.

prising since the two engines are essentially the same.

The view out front is good. The sharp ridge down the center of the hood is even more prominent from the driver's seat and proves useful for placing the car on the road. I'm a little cautious about pulling out from intersections. That long nose could get lopped off by oncoming traffic.

The cabin is an elegant place to be. The dark plastics and fabrics are richly grained, the carpet seems endless, and wood accents provide a nice contrast. It's formal yet cozy, rather like driving a gentleman's smoking lounge. The bucket seats fit like overstuffed high-back library chairs. The driver has a clean view of the instruments and an easy reach to the steering wheel and shifter.

Other ergonomics are a bit messier. It's a long stretch to controls on the dash, and adjusting the radio and heater would be nigh-impossible with the shoulder belt fastened. The horn is activated by a thin rubber ring around the inside perimeter of the steering wheel—a firm grip on the rim produces accidental honks. The wide C-pillars somewhat impede vision to the rear until you get in the habit of looking around them.

Ride quality is very good. The suspension handles bumps with a minimum of noise and movement. There's no hint of being thrown off line. Steering is easy

and, more importantly, communicative. Power steering of the era didn't always manage this trait. The brakes are terrific, powerful and easy to modulate, and frankly better than the modern Ford systems used on the Crown Victoria and Grand Marquis.

The Grandé's handling has a competent feel. I don't choose to push it very hard, relying instead the evaluation of *Car Life*'s editors:

"The advantage of the small engine shows up best in handling. The Grandé is balanced, reducing understeer from a habit to a tendency.... The Grandé responded instantly, on wet pavement or dry. If the front end of the car pointed toward the outside, a flick of the wrist

1969 Mustang

brought it back into line. The testers could apply power all the way around sweeping turns, or could cruise through, or could even brake at mid-turn, without drama. The Grandé's cornering power was higher than a luxury Ponycar is expected to have. Its handling, a quality distinct from cornering, was better than that."

That magazine test concluded by describing the Grandé as a pleasant car, "a dull mistress but a fine sister." After my experience with Miller's coupe, I think it would be more accurate to compare it to a high society hostess. The Grandé puts you immediately at ease. It is always entertaining, never alarming. And most of all, it exudes classiness. Despite its beer-budget origins, this Mustang really does have the champagne-caliber refinement of the best Thunderbirds. 🐎

Acknowledgments and Bibliography

Auto Dictionary, *John Edwards (HPBooks, 1993)*; Car Life, *"390 Mustang: No One Shouted 'Hold the Onions!'" (January 1967)*; Car Life, *"'69 Pony Cars," (October 1968)*; Car Life, *"When It Rains, the Mustang Grandé Glues Itself to the Road," (February 1969)*; Car Life, *"428 Mach 1: Best Mustang Yet and Quickest Ever," (March 1969)*; Car Life, *"Move Over World—Here's the Boss!" (July 1969)*; Car Life, *"Hey Look! We Tracked Down a Boss 302 Mustang," (September 1969)*; Car Life, *"Best Ponycar: Mustang Mach 1," (September 1969)*; Encyclopedia of American Cars From 1930, *auto editors of Consumer Guide (Publications International, 1993)*; Great Cars of the 20th Century, *Arch Brown and Richard Langworth (Publications International, 1991)*; Motor Trend, *"Ford's Going Things," (September 1969)*; Motor Trend, *"Mustang Makes It Happen," (September 1970)*; Standard Catalog of American Cars 1946-1975, *ed. John Gunnell (Krause, 1995)*

Special thanks to Doug Miller, Indianapolis, Indiana.

Above: *Ford created Grandé to be a luxury Mustang for the country club set and succeeded in hitting their market target.* **Right:** *Gently dished steering wheel offers modicum of safety protection.*

Mustang Grandé...
your first Mustang
made life more delicious, right?
So how about a second helping?

Sheer luxury. All planned to reflect your lavish mood. As you can see from its very handsome styling and attractive appointments, such as wire-style wheel covers, dual racing-style mirrors and neat two-tone narrow tape stripes, Grandé says here is the elegant Mustang.
The standard 200-cubic-inch, 7-main-bearing Six is a lean-muscled, smooth performer. For greater punch, choose the larger, brand-new, 4.1 Litre six-cylinder engine. Provides added go with traditional Six economy. More power? Pick the spirited 302-cubic-inch V-8. Or one of five other V-8's all the way up to 335 hp.
Go with the standard 3-speed manual shift, or specify the two-way transmission: SelectShift. It'll do the shifting automatically, or you can go through the gears manually. You can downshift to low or second gear for manual control on hills, or for the fun of going through the gears. Comes with a sporty floor-mounted T-bar shift lever.
Add a vinyl roof that looks like real leather — in either black or parchment. Nice touches outside. Now see what's in store for you inside— just turn the page.

8

9

1969 BOSS 429 MUSTANG

Mean As A Junkyard Dog

by Dave Emanuel
photos by Roy Query

I T IS early in April 1969. The bone-chilling cold of winter has finally subsided, and as the trees awaken from their seasonal dormancy, signs of new life are also visible in other quarters. Cars that were rarely seen haunting barren, snow-covered winter streets, are now rumbling along Main Street or parked at drive-ins. The streets are alive with the sounds of muffled power, screeching tires and free-revving engines. All the old standbys, cars with monikers like SS-396, GTO, Fairlane GT, Hemi, Z/28, 4-4-2, Mustang GT and Corvette have returned. All but one. Steve's old 1964 427 Galaxie, the one with two four-barrels that used to tear up the Chevelles and Fairlanes, is no-where to be seen. A rumor had been circulating that Steve had finally decided to sell it, but nobody seemed to know for certain.

As you mull over the fate of the in-famous Galaxie, you pull into the drive-in to chat with the other guys, but when the conversation turns to Steve and his car, everybody comes up with the same questioning look—they're really not sure what Steve is up to. Then, conversation stops abruptly as the sound of

spinning tires is heard off in the distance. As all heads turn toward the street, a flash of white streaks by. It looks like a new Mustang, but something isn't quite right—no Mustang ever sounded like that. The mean mechanical growl that accompanied the flash was that of a race engine. A *big* race engine.

Your curiosity piqued, you and a few friends jump into a car and drive off in search of the phantom white streak. You cruise up and down Main Street a few times, looking carefully along each intersecting side street, but nothing even remotely resembles the car that could have been the white flash. Disheartened, you return to the drive-in and as you pull off the street, you spot it. Parked off by itself, with a crowd surrounding it, is a brand new white Mustang. Atop the hood is a rather large air scoop. On the front fender, just behind the wheel well, are the words "Boss 429." And standing by the driver's door, with a broad smile on his face, is Steve. At

least one of the rumors was correct, he really did sell the old Galaxie.

S teve knew that his new Mustang was something special. If nothing else, the price on the window sticker told him that. How special was another story. In 1969, few people had an inkling that only 859 Boss 429s would be produced that year. (In 1970 the number dropped to 499 as the Boss 429 option was deleted mid-year.) The car was seen as simply a big brother to the Boss 302, but its origins and purpose were significantly different.

Seeking to increase its share of the highly revered youth market, Ford had been involved in a variety of motorsports. Early on, a 271-hp option, based on the 289-cubic-inch powerplant, had been offered to perk up the Mustang's performance image. But in an era when cubic inches were in vogue, the high-strung 289 with its mechanical lifters and poor low-speed torque appealed only to hard-core performance enthusiasts. The masses wanted a large, smooth running engine with relatively mild valve timing and easy to care for hydraulic tappets.

To that end, Ford added a 335-hp, 390 cubic-inch big block to the option list in 1967. The concept of shoe-horning a large powerplant into the Mustang's engine compartment had already been proved the previous year, when several machines powered by race-prepared 427 engines were campaigned in Factory Experimental drag racing classes. The amount of rework required to make room for the 427 made a regular production big block option unfeasible, but when the Mustang was redesigned for 1967, the engine compartment was purposely configured to allow assembly

line installation of the large "FE" series engines.

The 390 filled the bill nicely, but with the debut of Chevrolet's 396 Camaro option, the 390 Mustang was no longer a front runner. Ford countered by offering a 427 option rated at 390-hp, but it was subsequently deleted and replaced with a 428, rated no doubt with tongue-in-cheek, at 335-hp. When *Hot Rod* magazine tested the 428 Mustang, it discovered that the car would cover the quarter mile in 13.5 seconds and reach a speed of over 106 miles per hour. With that type of performance, a regular production Mustang was finally a force to be reckoned with.

In 1969, a restyled Mustang was given flash to accompany performance. The Mach I option, replete with side stripes and an air scoop sticking through a cutout in the hood, provided appropriate visual accompaniment to the sound

and feel of the 428. Having grown longer, wider and approximately 150 pounds heavier, the 1969 Mustang couldn't quite match the acceleration of the previous year's model, but it was still capable of sub-14 second quarter mile times.

With the 428 holding its own in drag strip competition, Ford management turned its attention to other types of auto racing. The company answered the challenge issued by Chevrolet's Z/28 with a Trans-Am road racer of its own—the Boss 302 Mustang (see *SIA #59*). Ford sales literature was brutally frank in describing the vehicle stating, "Powered by a five-liter (302 c.i.d.) F.I.A. formula engine aimed at the International Sedan Racing Class and the formula-oriented sportsman driver, the Boss 302 offers many unique features, as well as an array of special options not likely to be seen on any other street machine."

MUSTANG

Following the same philosophy, that of offering a "race it on Sunday, drive it to work on Monday" machine as a means of assuring homologation, Ford listed the Boss 429 as a mid-year option (in addition to, not in place of the 428). The major difference was that the 429/Mustang combination didn't really address the requirements of a particular category of racing as did the Boss 302. It was for Grand National competition that the 429 engine was best suited, but Fairlane rather than Mustang bodies were employed in that type of racing. NASCAR did sanction the powerplant for use in a Fairlane body, based on its being available in a Mustang, so Ford's purpose was served. But that left the Boss 429 as something of a bastard, a contender for the heavyweight championship with no place to fight. Except on the streets.

But it didn't really do well there. Being exceptionally nose heavy and fitted with an engine that produced a prodigious amount of torque, the Boss 429 lacked the type of traction required to win acceleration contests launched from traffic lights. Even when fitted with racing slicks, traction continually proved troublesome, a problem compounded by the engine's Lincoln Tunnel-sized ports which made for lazy rather than crisp throttle response. The less exotic 428 was actually a better street/drag performer.

Much of the problem with the 429 "Blue Crescent" or "Shotgun" engine (the latter sobriquet arising from the valve train configuration) was created by the very equipment that made it such a terror on a high-banked oval—the cylinder heads. Blessed with the largest ports ever used in an automotive application, the heads functioned somewhat like a pair of 20-inch biceps attached to the body of a 98-pound weakling—the potential for awe-inspiring power was there, but it couldn't be harnessed. When applied to anything other than a full-tilt race engine, the heads redefined the word "overkill." Of course, that followed rather naturally; the 429 "Blue Crescent" *was* a race engine.

Ford's concept with the "Shotgun" powerplant was to bring legitimacy to an engine which would offer the benefits of a hemispherical type combustion chamber and free-flowing intake and exhaust ports. To this end, the "Shotgun" cylinder head was given 2.40-inch and 1.90-inch exhaust valves in conjunction with an intake port diameter of 2.4375 inches. Reports of 429 engines producing in excess of 650-hp when equipped with a single 850 CFM Holley four-barrel carburetor were not uncommon. These vindicated Ford's belief

Above: Design of hood scoop is unique to the Boss 429. Right: Optional on other Mustangs, Magnum 500 wheels were standard on the Boss. Below: Battery was banished to the trunk because the engine bay was already filled with 429 cubic inches of fire and fury.

in the "Shotgun" as a race engine, but in detuning it for passenger car service, something was lost. Rated at 375-hp and 450 lbs./ft. torque, as installed in the Boss 429 Mustang, the detuned version of the engine simply never delivered on its promise.

Driving Impressions

The Boss 429 is a paradox. Mean as a junkyard dog one minute, it is as mild mannered as Clark Kent the next. A very quick car after the engine has made its initial ascent up the rpm scale, at low speeds performance is sluggish. The suspension has all the right ingredients for good handling, but in a corner the car leans as though a wheel had come off and the front end plows like a John Deere tractor. Overall, it's an appealing car, yet it has any number of annoying

quirks. Would I personally want to own one? Yes. And no.

With its unique valve train noises clearly audible through magnesium rocker arm covers, the Boss 429 works a magic all its own upon the ears. The sound of growling mechanicals up front superimposed on a distinctive exhaust note at the rear are aphrodisiacs to be savored in anticipation of an impending orgy of horsepower. Like a V-12 Ferrari, a Boss 429 has a sound all its own.

But—something happened on the way to the orgy. And if you have great expectations, you're in for a bit of a disappointment. From the driver's seat the large hood scoop dominates the forward view, serving notice that throbbing below is something more than a plebeian powerplant. That thought is reinforced by the placard on the dash which warns, "This vehicle is equipped with a manual choke located immediately below the

Far left: Rear seat head room and leg room are quite cramped. **Left:** *Space Saver spare adds a few more functional inches to already-small trunk.* **Below:** *Seat belts were standard, clipped into center console.* **Bottom:** *The 429 hemi; the closest thing to a grand national stock car engine that was street legal.*

ignition switch. For proper starting use manual choke." Adjacent to the choke knob is the hood scoop fresh air control—further evidence that driving a Boss 429 is serious business.

But in spite of indications to the contrary, the car's overall performance is significantly flawed. Given its cost, the priorities of the era in which it was built and Ford's marketing emphasis at the time—and that a Boss 429 was a specially constructed, almost hand-built vehicle—understanding the rationale behind many of the compromises made in the name of engineering is at best difficult. The engine is the biggest enigma. In seeking to tame the NASCAR fire-breather for passenger car service, compression ratio was lowered from 12.5:1 to 10.5:1, a mild hydraulic lifter cam was fitted, intake valve size was reduced and a Holley four-barrel rated at 735 CFM was utilized.

On paper, it all seems reasonable, but when you put the shift lever in first, release the clutch and caress the gas pedal, you find that the tiger doesn't exactly leap down the road. Much of the problem owes to cam timing which is simply too mild with respect to the colossal ports. The mismatch makes for poor part-throttle response, especially at low speeds. But as rpm builds, the engine begins its Dr. Jekyll to Mr. Hyde transformation. The junkyard dog begins to growl, bare its teeth and finally bite. As Rick Parker, owner of the car pictured here, phrases it, "It's a little sluggish at first, but once you get it above 3000 rpm the engine seems to really take over. When you get it out on the road and start cranking it through the gears, it's like a train; there's no stopping it—it really starts to come alive."

So long as the car is headed straight ahead, exercising the engine is tremendously enjoyable. Turning a corner

Internal Matters

Ford Motor Company began Boss 429 production on January 17, 1969, by installing a detour in the Mustang assembly line. The changes required to accommodate the 429 engine package were so extensive that the cars couldn't be constructed using normal mass production procedures. Instead, vehicles fitted with the 428 Super Cobra Jet engine were pulled from production and altered. Each of the parts to be deleted or added, from the 428 engine to such items as the "Rod-hood air scoop valve," were spelled out on a 35-page change order.

An indication of depth of the special work required to construct a Boss 429 is provided by the cover page of the change order entitled "Vehicle Release Conditions" which includes such items as:

1. This special high performance release package is intended to provide base vehicles for conversion by designated vendors as authorized by Special Vehicles Activity.

2. Vehicles built to these specifications are intended for interplant shipment only. Certification relative to compliance with F.M.V.S.S. H.E.W regulations on any vehicle incorporating this option must be furnished by Special Vehicles Activity prior to public sale.

3. Customer must be advised that warranty coverage is null and void on these vehicles except as extended by the Special Vehicles Activity.

4. This option released per the direction of Ford Car Product Planning Office product letter 69SF-260 dated 9-19-68.

5. Component design, system acceptability and engineering responsibility for vehicles incorporating this option remains with Special Vehicles Activity.

6. The D.S.O. activity has acted as agents only for special vehicles in release of this option to facilitate incorporation into Automotive Assembly Division build schedules.

7. Parts coded "X" in new part code column must be procured through Kar Kraft Purchasing activity.

specifications

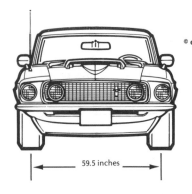

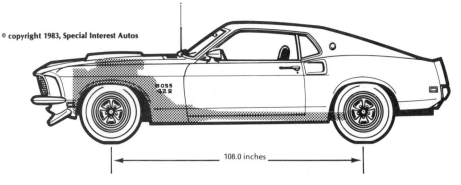

© copyright 1983, Special Interest Autos

59.5 inches

108.0 inches

1969 Boss 429 Mustang

Price $2740. As equipped: $4294.76

Optional equipment Boss 429 V-8 engine, high capacity engine oil cooler, 65 amp alternator, 85 amp trunk-mounted battery, power steering with oil cooler, 4-speed close ratio gearbox, power front disc brakes, rear drum brakes, Traction-lock rear axle, 3.91 ratio, special high performance suspension, front spoiler, F60-15 fiberglass belted tires, Magnum 500 15 x 7 chrome plated wheels, interior decor group, tachometer, console, high back bucket seats, dual racing mirrors, visibility group, deluxe seat belts.

ENGINE
Type	V-8 ohv
Bore and stroke	4.36 x 3.59
Displacement	429 cubic inches
Horsepower	375 at 5200 rpm
Torque	450 at 3400 rpm
Compression ratio	10.5:1
Induction system	Holley 735 CFM 4-bbl on aluminum manifold
Exhaust system	Dual, 2.25-inch diameter
Electrical system	12 volt battery/coil

TRANSMISSION
Type	4-speed manual, fully synchronized
Ratios: 1st	2.32:1
2nd	1.69:1
3rd	1.29:1
4th	1:1

DIFFERENTIAL
Type	Hypoid semi-floating, limited slip
Ratio	3.91:1

STEERING
Type	Semi reversible, recirculating ball, power assisted
Ratio	16.0:1
Turns lock to lock	3.7
Turning circle	37.6 feet

BRAKES
Type	Hydraulic with vacuum power assist, 11.3-inch diameter ventilated front discs, 10.0-inch diameter rear drums
Total swept area	282.5 square inches

CHASSIS AND BODY
Construction	Unit steel body welded to reinforced platform chassis
Body	2-door coupe

SUSPENSION
Front	Independent SLA, coil springs, double-acting tubular shocks, anti-sway bar
Rear	Live axle with semi-elliptic leaf springs, double acting tubular shocks (staggered mounting), anti-sway bar
Wheels	15-inch x 7-inch chromed steel
Tires	F60 x 15-inch Goodyear Polyglass

WEIGHTS AND MEASURES
Wheelbase	108.0 inches
Overall length	187.4 inches
Overall height	50.4 inches
Overall width	71.8 inches
Front tread	59.5 inches
Rear tread	59.5 inches
Curb weight	3716 pounds

PERFORMANCE
Maximum speed	130 plus (with 3.91:1 axle ratio)
Acceleration, 0-60	7.1 seconds
Standing start quarter mile	14.1 seconds and 102 mph
Fuel economy	10-14 mpg. Premium required

A bit sluggish off the mark, the 429 comes into its own at 3000 rpm and then runs like a Concorde at full throttle right past 130 mph.

Left: Oil cooler mounts in front of radiator, was standard equipment. Below left: High-back buckets up front, deluxe interior trim was also standard. Below center: Speedo reads to only 120 though car is quite capable of exceeding that figure with ease. Below: It's a long stretch to engage first gear.

MUSTANG

is another story. In spite of the trunk-mounted battery, aluminum cylinder heads, stiff suspension and stabilizer bars front and rear, front-end weight is so excessive that it leads to a tremendous amount of body roll and understeer. Pushing through a hard turn, the little voice inside you admonishes, "Keep up this nonsense and you're going to wreck this guy's car. How the hell are you going to explain *that* to Brownell. Now back off the gas, ease up on the steering wheel and get this thing straightened out." This is strange behavior, because understeer in a car with sufficient torque to bring the rear end around usually inspires all manner of heroics.

Even Parker, who has logged more than a few miles behind the wheel of a Boss 429 (this one and others) and is something of an expert on the cars, hears the little voice when he attempts a high speed turn. But there was another reason to avoid the hero driver stuff. Parker's Wimbledon White Boss is virtually a brand new automobile; the odometer shows less than 9500 miles.

As opposed to most low mileage cars which, if you can believe everything you hear, were originally purchased by little old ladies, Parker's Mustang was originally destined to be pressed into drag strip duty. The car, which was the sixty-eighth Boss 429 built (Boss 429 serial numbers began with 1200. Parker's car, which was built January 29, 1969, is numbered 1268) was purchased by the original owner in May 1969. After driving it 9027 miles, he

parked it, removed the engine, transmission and rear axle, and began preparing things for competition. Somewhere along the line either money, ambition or both ran out, dreams of being Top Eliminator faded and the car simply sat. And sat.

In 1979, while attending a local car show, Parker heard that a "hemi Mustang" was for sale. He went to see it and found, "it had mildew and mold (from sitting), but the car was in great shape." As a result, virtually all of the original equipment—from the wiper blades to the headlights—was (and is) still in place.

But the restoration process wasn't a particularly easy one. Parker says, "When I got it, the engine was in zillions of pieces—in fact, one guy told me the engine would never run again—so for about the first three weeks, all I did was to sort nuts, bolts and miscellaneous pieces of hardware. It took me about 18 months to reassemble the engine and reinstall it along with the transmission and rear end."

Ford Motor Company is currently telling the world that the Boss is back. That may be true, but there are bosses and there are BOSSES. And in spite of the previously noted imperfections in its character, the Boss 429 has that certain *je ne sais quoi* that sets it apart. Pretenders need not apply. □

Acknowledgements and Bibliography

Car Craft *magazine, various issues, 1969; PHR 1969 Engine annual;* Mustang—The Complete History of America's Ponycar *by Gary Witzenberg.*
Special thanks to Rick Parker, Columbus, Ohio, and Roy Query, Columbus Ohio.

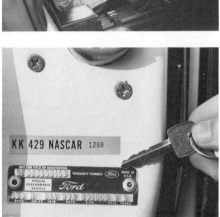

Above: The data plate that says it all. Below: Just your average Mustang, right? What about those dual pipes and the wide tires? They weren't added by some local leadfoot.

1969 Shelby GT 350

"A Thunderbird for Hell's Angels?"

by John F. Katz
photos by Vince Wright

BROCK Yates didn't think much of the '69 Shelby. "A garter snake in a Cobra skin," he sneered when, as Senior Editor at *Car and Driver*, he tested a GT 350 for the February 1969 issue. "A tough-looking Mustang Grande. A Thunderbird for Hell's Angels."

Certainly, the Shelby Mustang had evolved into a very different animal since its dramatic debut in January '65, when Carroll Shelby built a short run of white-and-blue fastbacks to homologate Ford's SCCA B/Production racing program. Class rules allowed non-homologated modifications to the engine *or* suspension but not both, so all 562 of the 1965 street models rolled out on racing chassis, with front ends lowered a full inch, rear traction bars that hooked up inside the body where the back seat should have been, and brutally stiff springs all around. "In all honesty," even *Car and Driver* allowed back in May '65, "it cannot be said that the Mustang GT 350 is the sort of car a sane man would enjoy driving at all times and under all conditions."

The '69 model was nothing like that, and that's probably why it disappointed Mr. Yates. But change isn't always for the worse. As a fast road car that could double as real-world transportation, the '69 GT 350 may have been the best Shelby Mustang, ever.

Of course, the '69 Shelby still *pretended* to be a racer, and the pretense no doubt aggravated its detractors. Before they could even get in the car, they'd have to deal with the double shoulder harnesses that bolted to the floor and then clipped to an inertia reel mounted on the internal roll bar. You have to wriggle into them, and they aren't particularly comfortable, although I probably could get used to them with time. Nonetheless, their safety advantage is obvious. John Kefalonitis, who owns our driveReport car and who *has* raced it, said that they hold him very well out on the track. Conventional lap belts supplement the shoulder harnesses for full four-point protection.

The shoulder belts unhook from the roll bar for easier access to the back seat, though why anyone would want to sit back there is beyond me. I suppose that getting the harnesses out of the way also makes it easier to fold the seat flat and stow luggage on top of it. That's certainly what I'd recommend.

Up front, however, the high-back buckets feel pretty fine, as does the relationship between the pedals and the pleasingly hefty, low-set steering wheel. But the wood-grained plastic on the wheel and shift handle doesn't even begin to simulate the real thing; and the inherited Mustang dashboard harbors lots of hard, flashy materials and a strained shape that sweeps most accessory controls out of easy reach. The instrument markings are too fine for legibility (an affectation shared with GM cars of the same era), and the steer-

ing wheel scores an anti-ergonomic grand slam by cutting across the most critical range of the temperature gauge, speedometer, tachometer, *and* fuel gauge. Shelby added oil and amp gauges angled toward the driver, GT-40 style, but put them too low on the console for easy reading. And speaking of not seeing things, the Mustang "Sports Roof" effectively hides anything that might be approaching from the right rear quarter.

John's GT 350 packs a Paxton-McCulloch centrifugal supercharger—a rare and controversial option that we'll discuss in a sidebar—feeding the 351 Windsor that served as Shelby's base engine in '69. The car idles with a boisterous, lumpy rhythm and anxiously lurches forward the instant the T-handle shifter hits "Drive." At this point I still anticipated the standard muscle-car experience, with much balking and hesitation at low speed, followed by a terrific kick in the pants as the engine climbed up on top of its steep cam timing. But the supercharged Shelby is nothing like that; hardly had I dipped a toe into the accelerator, when the rollicking vibrations smooth over into a liquid flow of torque, building relentlessly with the rising whistle of the blower, and interrupted only by the perceptible, but not uncomfortable, shifting of the trans-

mission—from a walking speed until we ran out of runway at 90 mph. The acceleration is seamless, and speed is deceptive: 50 mph feels like 25, and 90 seems like 60, until you glance down and see just how far you've wound the needle 'round the 140-mph speedometer. It makes the Shelby less amusing as a toy, perhaps, but more effective as a tool.

Still, by '69 the Shelby chassis shared more pieces with the Mach 1 Mustang than with a B/Production champion. Yates complained of extreme rough-road instability, due at least in part to the flexible platform of his convertible test car. I noticed no such untoward behavior in John's Sports Roof coupe, and we did hit some fairly rough roads, though probably not as fast as *C/D*'s test regimen would have required. I do agree that Ford's overboosted power steering compromises road feel. But I'd add that the Shelby responds sharply and predictably to the helm, and that it carves through corners flat and neutral, with the power on or off. It rides on most surfaces with a tightly controlled but civilized demeanor. The touchy brakes grabbed unpredictably when they were cold, but grew smoother as I used them, although the pedal remained soft and numb.

Whatever its flaws, the '69 GT 350 is,

on the whole, a satisfying automobile, combining the boyish exuberance of the most outlandish pony cars with a level of refinement usually reserved for mid-size muscle machines. But as we said before, that's not the way the Shelby Mustang started out.

Carroll Shelby was busy racing Cobras in the summer of '64, when Ford Division chief Lee Iacocca asked him to build and campaign road-racing Mustangs as well. Winning ranked higher than styling, although Shelby did create a distinctive look by juggling some trim and adding bold blue stripes and a functional hood scoop. The top Mustang engine was a solid-lifter 289 rated 271 bhp; Shelby added a 715-cfm Holley four-barrel breathing down an aluminum high-rise manifold, tubular exhaust headers, and other tweaks that bumped its output up to 306 horses — and that was in street tune.

Shelby has always insisted that the GT 350 badge stood for nothing more significant than the distance (in feet) between his Venice, California, factory and the building directly across the road. Ford officials wanted to call the car "Mustang Cobra" and were grappling with the chimeric hybrid of *Equus* and *Serpentinus* that would imply as a logo. Bored with a meeting on subject,

1969 Shelby

Ol' Shel asked chief engineer Phil Remington to pace off the distance between the buildings. Of course, it couldn't have hurt that "350" implied both more horsepower and more cubic inches than the street-edition Shelby Mustang really offered — although, to be fair, the full-race GT 350R probably did develop between 325 and 360 ponies.

But a racer by any other name still runs as fast. By the end of the season Shelby had built 37 R-models and captured the B/Production championship — out-running E-Type Jaguars, Porsche 904s and small-block Corvettes. SCCA required only 100 road-going GT 350s for homologation, but Shelby assembled five times as many to meet buyer demand. Many of those were converted to R-specification. It wasn't hard to do.

Shelby could have stopped right there and, left to his own inclination, he probably would have. He had placed enough

Ford Mustang Production, 1965-70

	1965	1966	1967	1968	1969	1970
GT 350R	37					
GT 350 fastback	562	1,438	1,175	1,253	1,085	260
GT 350H		1,000				
GT 350 convertible		6		404	94	57
GT 500 fastback			2,050	1,140	1,536	382
GT 500 convertible				402	335	90
GT 500KR fastback				933		
GT 500KR convertible				318		
TOTAL for year	599	2,444	3,225	4,450	3,150	789

Notes: All 1969-70 GT 500s were tuned to the previous year's GT 500KR specifications, but lacked the KR label. "1970" models were actually leftover '69s, freshened up with new hood stripes.

Left: Taillamps actually do look more T-Bird than Mustang. **Below:** Quad exhaust tips give fair warning of performance potential. **Bottom:** With all its stripes, ducts and add-ons it looks a mobile menace.

racing Mustangs into circulation to keep on winning for some time; in fact, '65 Shelbys would capture the B/Production title again in 1966 and '67. But Ford wanted more production Shelbys to promote the Mustang's high-performance image. And Shelby, who enjoyed his involvement with Ford's racing program, wanted to keep the boys in Dearborn happy.

The SCCA introduced the Trans Am series in March 1966, and Shelby-campaigned Mustangs won it, too, as they would again in '67. Shelby took over development of Ford's road-racing GT-40 and leased a pair of aircraft hangars at Los Angeles International to expand his shop space. He ended Cobra production, partly to make room for more Mustangs.

The first 252 1966 GT 350s were mildly restyled and mechanically identi-

Ford's Horse Race in 1969
Who built the hottest Mustang?

	Boss 302	GT 350	Mach 1 CJ	GT 500	Boss 429
Base price	$2,740	$4,434	$3,479	$4,700	N/A
Bore x stroke, inches	4 x 3	4 x 3.5	4.13 x 3.98	4.13 x 3.98	4.36 x 3.59
C.i.d.	302	351	428	428	429
Compression	10.5:1	10.7:1	10.6:1	10.7:1	10.5:1
Bhp @ rpm	290 @ 5,800	290 @ 4,800	335 @ 5,200	335 @ 5,200	375 @ 5,200
Torque (lb-ft) @ rpm	290 @ 4,300	385 @ 3,200	440 @ 3,400	440 @ 3,400	450 @ 3,400
Valve lifters	Mechanical	Hydraulic	Hydraulic	Hydraulic	Mechanical
Carb, cfm	780	550	735	735	735
Curb weight, lb.	3,387	3,600	3,607	3,850	3,400
Distribution, f/r	56/44	55/45	59/41	57/43	56/44
Bhp/c.i.d.	0.96	0.82	0.78	0.78	0.87
Lb/bhp	11.7	12.4	10.7	11.5	9.1
Performance					
0-60 mph, seconds	6.0	N/A	5.7	6.0	5.3
0-100, seconds	15.2	N/A	14.3	13.9	N/A
1/4 mile @ mph	14.6 @ 97.6	N/A	14.3 @ 100	14.0 @ 102	12.3@112
Source:	C/D June '69	N/A	C/D November '68	SCG February '69	MT April '70*

*Test car had blueprinted engine and mildly modified chassis

illustrations by Russell von Sauers, The Graphic Automobile Studio

specifications

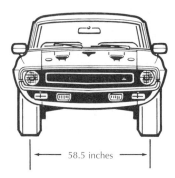

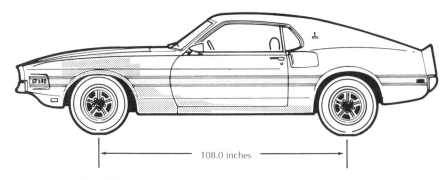

58.5 inches

108.0 inches

1969 Shelby GT 350

Price	$4,434
Std. equipment inc.	Power steering, power front disc brakes, deluxe interior with imitation teak trim, high-back vinyl bucket seats, four-point inertia reel safety belts
Options on dR car	Paxton centrifugal supercharger, automatic transmission, Traction-Loc, AM radio with eight-track, aluminum wheels, "Sport Deck" folding rear seat, tinted glass
Price as equipped	$5,265 (est.)

ENGINE

Type	V-8
Bore x stroke	4.00 inches x 3.50 inches
Displacement	351 cubic inches
Compression ratio	10.7:1
Bhp @ rpm (est.)	390 @ 3,700
Torque @ rpm (est.)	515 @ 3,400
Taxable horsepower	51.2
Valve gear	Ohv
Valve lifters	Hydraulic
Main bearings	5
Induction system	Paxton centrifugal supercharger feeding one Autolite 4-bbl carb
Fuel system	Mechanical pump
Lubrication system	Pressure, gear-type pump
Cooling system	Pressure, centrifugal pump
Exhaust system	Dual sharing single transverse muffler
Electrical system	12-volt

TRANSMISSION

Type	3-speed planetary automatic with hydraulic torque converter

Ratios: 1st	2.40:1
2nd	1.47:1
3rd	1.00:1
Reverse	2.00:1
Max. torque converter	2.02:1

DIFFERENTIAL

Type	Hypoid, semi-floating, limited slip
Ratio	3.25:1

STEERING

Type	Recirculating ball with hydraulic servo
Turns lock-to-lock	3.8
Ratios	16.1:1 gear; 20.3:1 overall
Turning diameter	37.4 feet (curb/curb)

BRAKES

Type	4-wheel hydraulic with vacuum servo
Front	11.3- inch vented disc
Rear	10 x 2.00-inch drum
Swept area	341 square inches
Parking brake	Mechanical, on rear wheels

CHASSIS & BODY

Construction	Platform frame with integral body
Body	Welded steel stampings
Body style	2+2 fastback coupe

SUSPENSION

Front	Independent, upper A-arms, lower strut-stabilized arms, coil springs, link-type anti-roll bar
Rear	Live axle on asymmetric leaf springs
Shock absorbers	Gabriel adjustable telescopic
Tires	Goodyear Speedway E70 x 15
Wheels	Alloy center with steel rim, 7 x 15

WEIGHTS AND MEASURES

Wheelbase	108 inches
Overall length	190.6 inches
Overall width	71.8 inches
Overall height	N/A
Front track	58.5 inches
Rear track	58.5 inches
Min. road clearance	N/A
Shipping weight	3,600 pounds (w/out options)
Distribution f/r	55/45

CAPACITIES

Crankcase	4 quarts (less filter)
Cooling system	16.5 quarts
Fuel tank	20 gallons
Transmission	N/A
Rear axle	4.5 pints

CALCULATED DATA

Horsepower per c.i.d.	1.11
Weight per hp	6.7 pounds
Lb./sq. in. brakes	10.6
Stroke/bore ratio	.875:1

1969 Shelby

cal to the '65s. But after that, Dearborn began to dictate a more "cost-effective" approach. The Shelby's sintered metallic brake linings and modified steering linkage remained, but the front suspension returned to its stock height. In the rear, Ford forced Shelby to abandon the custom-made traction bars in favor of aftermarket Traction Masters—which in turn allowed an optional rear seat.

Urged on by Ford, Shelby tried to broaden his pony's appeal by offering an automatic transmission, and by consigning the noisy Detroit Locker rear to the option list. Red, blue, green, and black joined white on the color chart. A special run of 1,000 "GT 350H" models, most of them black with gold stripes, were delivered to the Hertz rent-a-car company; Hertz had previously rented Corvettes, before switching its allegiance from GM to Ford.

On the positive side, Shelby's parts catalog now presented a Paxton centrifugal supercharger; $435 bought not only the blower but all of the necessary belts and brackets, plus a tough-looking cast carburetor enclosure with a black pebble finish and "Cobra" in raised white letters. The catalog optimistically listed installation time as six hours and claimed a 46 percent(!) boost in horsepower. Curiously, Shelby did not specify reduced compression with the blower. But the installation did void Ford's extended powertrain warranty.

By 1967, the Shelby's transformation from ready road racer to plush premium Mustang was nearly complete. Even the Traction Masters were gone, replaced by rubber snubbers on smoother-riding springs. Koni shocks gave way to still-adjustable but softer and domestically produced Gabriels. Heavy-duty brake linings replaced the all-out racing material used previously. Conceivably, an adventurous owner could still take a '67 GT 350 racing, but few did. Shelby was playing to a new audience, one that preferred power steering, power brakes, and automatic transmission. Many '67s had air conditioning, too.

Dearborn wanted a more distinctive appearance, preferably with minimal cost and effort. Designers Chuck McHose and Peter Stacey were dispatched to L.A., along with a stripped-out Mustang body shell to use as a styling buck. The body was a real mess, having been wrecked in a seat-belt test. Shelby himself suggested a three-inch-longer nose and quad headlights, with the inboard units set in a deeply recessed grille. McHose and Stacey worked out the details in clay directly over the sheet metal wreck. For the rear, they wanted '65 Thunderbird taillights, but Ford made them take '67 Cougar units instead. A full-width fiberglass spoiler and a generous sprinkling of fiberglass scoops completed the '67 Shelby look. Unfortunately, the fiberglass pieces fit poorly, possibly because local suppliers weren't all that sophisticated, or maybe because the parts had been designed on a body that wasn't quite straight.

Ford offered a 315-bhp 390 in the '67 Mustang GT, so to stay on top Shelby launched the GT 500, packing a 428 topped off with twin 600-cfm Holleys. The big engine delivered easy torque and domesticated flexibility that the high-strung small-block just couldn't match—but at the expense of handling.

At 3,286 pounds, the GT 500 still weighed less than a Corvette, but its 56/44 weight distribution guaranteed that it would never be taken seriously as a road racer.

But if Shelbys were no longer racers, they were still serious performers. *Sports Car Graphic* recorded a top speed of 129 mph for the '67 GT-350, which was five mph higher than *Road & Track* had measured for a '65 model with the same 3.89:1 gears. Handling suffered less than expected, thanks to two inches more track and Ford's own refinements to the donor Mustang's chassis. The GT 500 neither rode nor handled as well as its small-block stablemate—but it could top 130.

Then the airport decided not to renew Shelby's lease, as a more "airport-related" business had bid on the buildings. Ford relocated Shelby assembly to A.O. Smith in Ionia, Michigan, for lower costs and closer scrutiny. Despite this major disruption, Shelby still managed to produce 3,225 cars for the model year.

Fiberglass quality improved dramatically for '68, because Smith invested in matched metal dies to mold the parts more precisely. Single headlamps returned, balanced by rectangular Lucas driving lights in the grille. A bigger hood scoop sat further forward on the hood, where aerodynamic testing had shown it would do the most good. Around back, the Cougar taillights gave way to the Thunderbird units that the designers wanted all along.

The '68 GT 350 was considerably

This page: A cockpit full of Cobras; on the shifter, the sports steering wheel, even the window cranks! *Facing page:* Engine develops 39 more horses than it has cubic inches.

1969 Shelby

tamed, powered by a hydraulic-lifter 302 developing only 250 bhp at 4,800 rpm. With the supercharger, Shelby now claimed a more realistic 335-bhp at 5,200. The GT 500 began the year powered by the same dual-quad 428. But in mid-season Ford released the deeper-breathing 428 CJ-R (for Cobra Jet-Ram air), very conservatively underrated at 335 bhp with a single 735-cfm carb. Shelby switched over to the new engine in April, and at the same time added the suffix KR (for King of the Road) to the GT 500 label. His operation closed the year

A Supercharged '69 Shelby?

Sharp Shelby fans already know that Carroll didn't offer a supercharger kit in 1969. But our driveReport car is one of two blown '69s known to the Shelby American Automobile Club (SAAC).

John Kefalonitis theorizes that the Paxton blower is a dealer modification. The installation on his car is identical to a 1966-68 factory job, and of course there was nothing to prevent an enterprising service manager from ordering the parts and bolting them on a '69. But John hasn't found a way to document his theory.

The blower was on the car when he bought it in 1994, from a collector-car dealer in Lakewood, New Jersey. At that time the Shelby carried an Arizona title, but John was able to trace its history back to Town and Country Ford of Rockport, Illinois. Unfortunately, Town and Country had since packed up and relocated to Charlotte, North Carolina, where they are thriving today. If they have any relevant service records left from Rockport days, they are all crated, and no one is in any hurry to uncrate them. John knows, he's asked.

There is, of course, another possibility. Like most small-scale specialty builders, Shelby wasn't against using up last year's parts on this year's models, and if he happened to have a supercharger or two still in the box, well. . . . John has taken the question to the great man himself, who simply scratched his head and admitted that he didn't remember.

John didn't buy his Shelby as a show car, anyway; he bought it to race with SAAC. Previous owners had chromed a fair portion of the engine bay and then allowed the car to deteriorate to mediocre condition. But John gradually stripped off the non-authentic gewgaws and eventually repainted the body its original Acapulco Blue. The upholstery—black vinyl with red trim, a combination also available on deluxe-interior Mustangs—remains original. The alternator is still chromed, only because John hasn't gotten around to replacing it yet.

After a few years of restoration, he no longer wanted to risk the car on the track. So he bought a '69 Mach 1 428CJ for racing and retired his snake to show duty. The

Shelby won an AACA First Junior award in 1997, and has since collected Senior and Preservation trophies from AACA as well as a Silver Award from the Mustang Club of America.

Interestingly, John told us that the blown 351 actually pulls stronger at the low end than his 428 Cobra Jet—and that the extra flexibility never hurt his lap times. And while the Mach 1 will outrun the Shelby at the top end, the difference isn't as great as you might expect.

Furthermore, the additional weight of the 428, noticeable on the street, turns into an anchor on the track. The Mach 1 blunders into corners and thunders out of them; the GT 350 slickly slithers through.

Ironically, Shelby could have promoted the supercharged 351 as a real alternative to the Ford-badged Mustangs—combining big-block Cobra Jet performance with small-block Boss 302 roadability. The cost could hardly have mattered. What did matter is that Carroll Shelby wanted to get out of the Mustang business, and by 1969 nothing was going to stop him.

with 4,450 sales, a healthy 37 percent increase over '67.

For '69, Ford finally gave Shelby styling the attention it deserved. The Design department created literally hundreds of preliminary drawings, dozens of scale models, and more than one full-scale plaster. In the end, only the roof, doors, and rear quarters were shared with the Mustang; Owens-Corning provided 21 separate fiberglass pieces to complete the rest of outer skin. The '69 Shelby's full-width grille predicted the look of the new-generation Mustang for '71, and its functional front-fender brake ducts would reappear a year later on the Mustang Milano show car. So would the Shelby's new hood, which looked as though it had been attacked with a giant church key. No fewer than four openings provided auxiliary underhood cooling, while a NACA duct in the center actually fed the air cleaner. Wire screens behind the openings kept out wildlife and debris. The Lucas fog lamps moved out of the grille and down below the bumper. The quartz-iodine bulbs needed to make them truly effective were still illegal, but were easy enough to install when no one was looking.

Rear brake scoops—up high on the shoulders of fastbacks, down on the quarter panel on convertibles—were supposedly functional but only blew air on the tires. Around the back, the Thunderbird taillights remained but now two large, rectangular exhaust outlets exited the center of the valence below the bumper. *Sports Car Graphic* called the '69 Shelby "a paragon of what Shelby cars should have looked like five years ago, instead of being Mustang mutants covered with scoops that stuck out like warts on a witch's nose."

Convertibles featured a unique vinyl boot that fastened without snaps. Sadly, the roll bars on both coupes and convertibles were no longer functional, being much thinner and bolted to the body sides rather than the floor. But the fiberglass parts were thick and sturdy, designed more for durability than light weight. The 'glass front fenders and hood saved 20 pounds over the stock sheet metal, but the completed car weighed a whopping 3,600 pounds.

Again Shelby switched to a larger engine for the GT 350, this time to the 351 produced in Windsor, Ontario. Conceptually, this was just a 302 with a still-longer stroke, and in Shelby tune, with a 550-cfm Autolite carburetor and aluminum high-rise manifold, it rated 290 bhp at 3,400 rpm and 385 foot pounds of torque at 3,200.

The 335-bhp CJ-428 continued as the power plant for the GT 500, although Shelby dropped the "KR" suffix. GT 350s were offered with a choice of close or wide-ratio four speeds or with Cruise-O-Matic; GT 500s came only with the auto-

matic or a close-ratio manual. Air conditioning could be ordered on 350s with any of the three transmissions but only on automatic 500s. The Traction-Lok differential remained available on any Shelby that didn't have air conditioning. Mid-way through the model year, F60 x 15 tires replaced E70 x 15s. By this time Shelbys came painted in the full range of Mustang colors, with interiors offered in white, black, or—according to some sources—red by the end of the season. Luminous side stripes could be ordered in blue, gold, black, or white. A special pink Sports Roof model was presented to *Playboy*'s Playmate of the Year; some sources say that replicas of this car were available to the fully clothed public, but this seems doubtful.

The Shelbys the public could buy were usually fully loaded. Since the cars were relatively scarce, the dealers who could get them tended to order them with every conceivable option. Thus equipped, a GT 500 convertible might list for $6,300—more than the racing GT 350R had commanded back in '65. And at that price, there were few takers.

Even the press had lost interest—or maybe Ford just wasn't bothering to include Shelbys in the press fleet any more. Yates's diatribe in *Car and Driver* was the only contemporary test of a '69 GT 350 that we could find. *Sports Car Graphic* tested a GT 500, raved about its new looks and refinement but castigated it for its fading brakes and nose-

Clubs and Specialists

Shelby American Automobile Club
P.O. Box 788
Sharon, CT 06069
Fax: (860) 364-0769

Mustang Club of America Inc.
3588 Hwy. 138, Suite 365
Stockbridge, GA 30281
770-477-1965

Mustang Owners Club International
2720 Tennessee NW
Albuquerque, NM 87110
505-296-2554

Tony D. Branda
1434 E. Pleasant Valley Blvd.
Altoona, PA 16602
800-458-3477

Mustangs & More
2065 Sperry Ave., No. C
Ventura, CA 93003
805-642-0887

Classic Mustang Parts of Oklahoma
8801 S. Interstate 35
Oklahoma City, OK 73149
800-706-8801

Mustangs Unlimited
185 Adams St.
Manchester, CT 06040
860-647-1965

Larry's T-Bird & Mustang Parts
511 S. Raymond Ave.
Fullerton, CA 92831
800-854-0393

Auto Krafters
522 S. Main St.
Broadway, VA 22815
540-896-5910

Canadian Mustang
20529 62 Ave.
Langley, BC, Canada V3A 8R4
604-534-6424

Mostly Mustangs
55 Alling St.
Hamden, CT 06517
203-562-8804

The Paddock
221 West Main
Knightstown, IN 46148
800-428-4319

1969 Shelby

heavy handling. The editors did allow that the '69 model was improved over the "canine" '68 GT 500KR.

But if Carroll Shelby had gone from building the fastest Mustangs to the flashiest, at least he was doing a better job of it than ever before. Unfortunately, that was no longer enough. By 1969, Ford dealers offered the Mustang Mach 1, which was fast *and* flashy and, even packing the CJ 428, cost $1,200 less than a GT 500. The new Boss 429, whatever its flaws, seemed destined to carry Ford's banner in drag racing. In the Trans Am series, it was the Ford-developed Boss 302 that was chasing the Z/28 Camaros. And while the Chevys would dominate on the track, *Car and Driver* called the road-going Boss "easily the best Mustang yet — and that includes *all* the Shelbys. . . ."

Carroll knew his cars had run out of *raison d'être*. Tired of dealing with the bureaucracy in Dearborn, and wary of the new regulations coming from Washington, he left Ford to sell wheels and accessories. Ford retained the right to use the Cobra name — and did they ever. Leftover '69 Shelbys were embellished with hood stripes and a unique chin spoiler and re-serialed as 1970 models. ◌

Left: Shelby's corporate signature. **Above:** *Speedo holds great promise of rapid transit.* **Below left:** *Cover leaves no doubt what car it belongs to.* **Bottom:** *Rare Paxton supercharger option makes a fast car even faster.*

Bibliography and Acknowledgments

Books: John A. Gunnell (editor) Standard Catalog of American Cars 1946-1975; *Jay Lamm and Nick Nicaise,* Illustrated Shelby Buyer's Guide; *Gary L. Witzenburg,* Mustang, the Complete History of America's Pioneer Ponycar; *Wallace A. Wyss,* Shelby's Wildlife — The Cobras and the Mustangs.

Periodicals: Dave Emanuel, "1966 Mustang Shelby GT 350H," SIA #78 and "1968 Shelby GT 500-KR," SIA #83; Jerry Titus, "Shelby Mustang GT 350 & GT 500," Sports Car Graphic, March 1967; Brock Yates, "Shelby GT 350," Car and Driver, February 1969; "Shelby's Lunch Wagon," SCG, February 1969.

Thanks to Vinny Liska of SAAC; Kim M. Miller of the AACA Library and Research Center; Mike Petruska of Blairstown Airport; Henry Siegle. Special thanks to owners John and Barbara Kefalonitis.

Owning One

John and Barbara Kefalonitis bought a Shelby when they "got kind of bored" with their '56 T-Bird. "We went and looked at a '65 396 Corvette, but it turned out to be bogus. And then we saw this, and the deal was right."

The car is unique. According to the Shelby American Automobile Club (SAAC), it was the only '69 GT 350 built with its particular combination of colors and options. And that's *before* the supercharger was installed.

The club is both active and helpful. "We have enjoyed SAAC immensely," John told us. "We take a car to the track once a year to race with them. We've raced at Charlotte, Road America, Lime Rock, and Atlanta, and we're not sure where we're going next year. But when they have a Shelby convention, they make sure you get two to three days of track time. Sometimes there's even a driving school."

Around half of the Shelby Mustangs built in 1967-70 survive; the rate is slightly higher for '65-66 models. Vinny Liska, SAAC's representative in New Jersey, estimated that a well-restored GT 350 would

sell in the mid-twenties, with a GT 500 commanding closer to $30,000. The '69 models aren't worth nearly as much as the '65–66 cars but hold their own against '67s and usually top the more plentiful '68s. All Shelby Mustangs are appreciating, but slowly; and as with anything else these days, your best deal is a car that's already restored.

"The most important thing to do," said John, "is to get hold of someone with a registry, so you can check the serial number. It's over 1,300 pages of strictly Shelbys. Then you can call whoever is in charge of the year and model, and they can pick out everything and anything on that particular car. I looked at a convertible down in West Virginia, and the guy said it was Acapulco Blue. But Vinny cross-referenced the serial number in his computer, and it turned out it was originally Grabber Green."

Another word of caution: Shelby installed fiberglass engine hoods using the factory Mustang hardware. But the hood springs are much too stiff for the lightweight material, and the 'glass tends to bow when the hood is closed. John removed the springs

and put in a prop rod, which is all the lightweight hood needs, anyway.

The Illustrated Shelby Buyer's Guide, by Jay Lamm and Nick Nicaise, is another excellent resource. Among other things, it advises '69 Shelby owners to use only the correct, non-vented gas gap. On the big-block GT 500s, heat from the centrally mounted exhaust can ignite fumes from a vented gas cap. Mid-way through '69, Ford recalled the entire run of GT 500s to install non-vented caps and a new vent system that emptied through a hose under the car. GT 350s were never affected.

The exhausts still corrode the bumper plating, but there isn't much you can do about that.

The '69 Shelby interior is virtually all stock Mustang, except for the seat belts, console, and various Shelby and Cobra emblems. Unfortunately, many of these Shelby-specific gewgaws weren't that well glued on, and they tend to fall off.

John himself sells hoses, decals, belts, wiring, data plates, and manuals for Mustangs and Shelbys, through B&J Specialties, in Blairstown, New Jersey.

1970 MUSTANG BOSS 302

Dearborn's Camaro-Eater

by Jerry Heasley

T HE LAST rose of summer. That's what Jacques Passino of Ford racing fame called the Boss 302. "The engine and the car did more than we could have expected it to do. It was a winner, it was a good car, a good street machine. But I guess you could call it the last rose of summer, because right after that, everything died."

By any measure, the Boss 302 was a success. It accomplished for Ford about everything they asked of it. It won on the Trans-Am circuit, and on the street it improved the performance image of the Mustang. But the days of the high-performance production car, specially produced to make a car eligible for racing, were ending for Ford Motor Company. With the Boss, Ford left with a winner.

But let's back up a few years, at least to 1963. By this date, Ford was involved

in perhaps the most ambitious, far-flung racing program in the history of motor sport. The company itself was worldwide, and so was the racing effort. By 1966 Ford's successes were legion. In that year, they copped the World Manufacturer's championship, the Indianapolis 500 and the SCCA Trans-Am sedan racing championship. They were competing on a massive scale, flexing their muscles from NASCAR to LeMans, from Trans-Am to Indianapolis, from international rallying to drag racing. They were everywhere, and they were awesome.

In 1967, however, Chevrolet introduced the new Camaro. By mid-model year they had a package for the street and track called the Z/28 (see SIA #53). Chevy was a couple of years behind with a ponycar, but they leaped ahead with a new "Z" car that could blow the doors

off any stock Mustang in town, and which became invincible in Trans-Am racing in 1968 and 1969. Now it was Ford that had to play catch-up. Ford had been on top of Trans-Am in 1966 and 1967, and by mid-1968 they were busy readying a package for the Mustang that would soon compete with the Z/28. The goal was to regain superiority in Trans-Am, and also field a Mustang on the street that was quicker, or at least as quick as the Z/28. It was so obvious that the Boss 302 was in the image of the Z/28 that one engineer at Ford laughingly told us that during its development he thought of the Boss as the "Z/29."

Who built job #1? How did it get off the ground? It was Kar Kraft of Special Vehicles, a contracted facility of Ford that built the first mechanical prototype. According to Don Eichstaedt of

Originally published in Special Interest Autos #59, Sept.-Oct. 1980

Ford Engineering, "Kar Kraft built the first prototype at about the same time they were building the prototype of the Boss 429. These were presented to management, and the decision was made for Kar Kraft, Special Vehicles to build, engineer, test and release the Boss 429 out at their Brighton assembly plant. Concurrently, they turned the Boss 302 over to Ford Engineering to be released as a 1969½ model, and it went through the regular Ford engineering process. But Special Vehicles did develop and build the first mechanical prototype for Knudsen's approval."

The Shinoda-inspired graphics were put on the car after it came from Special Vehicles and before it was presented to Knudsen. Once the prototype was approved, Boss 302 then became a regular production car and the specifications were turned over to Ford engineering.

However, the racing Boss 302 Mustangs were constructed at Kar Kraft. We talked with Chuck Mountain of Kar Kraft, who recalled that over an approximately two-year span they built 15 to 18 cars for competition. What were the differences in these vehicles, compared to the production 302s? According to Chuck, just about everything. The engines and drivelines were prepared by either Carroll Shelby or Bud Moore—whichever team the car went to. Major mods were done to the body at Kar Kraft. Chuck told us, "since the Mustang had a unitized body, a roll cage was built for a combination of safety and function." The roll cage increased the "torsional and bending stiffness of the vehicle, as well as adding protection for the driver." Of course, front and rear suspension, steering, brakes—everything was tweaked for competition, including the car's aerodynamics. The rear suspension used a Watts linkage with the solid axle. For better laminar air flow, the fake air scoops atop the rear quarters of the 1969 fastback were omitted. As Don Eichstaedt commented later, "they

1. Front spoiler came as standard equipment on Boss. 2. Mag-style wheels added to its street racer appearance. 3. Black headlight surrounds added to no-nonsense appearance up front. 4. "Speed stripe" was created by Larry Shinoda. 5. Adjustable rear spoiler was an option.

Boss 302 owners pay a price for that swoopy fastback styling. With rear seat up trunk space is tiny, even with space saver spare tire adding a few extra inches.

The Boss 302 in Trans-Am

"We should have won it in 1969, but we had some problems. The car was quick enough, as a matter of fact, between Parnelli and I [Parnelli Jones and George Follmer], we were sitting on the pole...We got beat in the pits a couple of times—not because of our crews—but because we had to make some extra pit stops...We had a series of bad tires for a while. We were both on Firestones. It kept us off the victory stand for a while."

Those were some comments from George Follmer, who, along with Parnelli Jones, Sam Posey, Peter Revson and Dan Gurney, raced Boss 302 Mustangs in pursuit of the 1969 Trans-Am sedan racing championship. After the first five races of 1969, it looked like Ford might dominate the pack. They led in points with 42, compared to Chevy's 30, and had four first place finishes to their credit. Their one second place finish was close—with Jones 13 seconds behind Ron Bucknum's Camaro. Then the problems came. Chevrolet clinched the championship on the eleventh race, at the Sears Point Trans-Am in Sonoma, California, on September 21, 1969.

In 1970, however, Ford turned it around, and got back to their winning ways of 1966 and 1967. It was Jones, Jones, Follmer and Jones winning the first four outings, and Ford coasted the rest of the way to the championship. In fact, AMC ended up in second place in the standings that year, beating Chevy by 19 points.

We talked to Larry Shinoda about the racing Boss 302s, and discovered a very interesting point. According to Larry, in 1970, "they finally spent more time with the suspension. The 302 had a front spoiler, but back in '69 the racing guys wouldn't use a rear spoiler at all. They were saying it would not work—they didn't need it. So, in 1969 they didn't use the bolt-on rear wing spoiler—although it was homologated for the car! Then, in 1970 they used front and rear spoilers; in fact, they finally got to the point where they would kick it [rear wing] all the way up at times. But, at a track like Riverside, they would run it at a fairly normal angle."

Ford had worked out the bugs for the '70 seasons and brought home the championship. But it was, as Passino said, "the last rose of summer," because factory support and factory money were gone in 1971.

For 1971, Follmer told us that he "ran a car in the same configuration of the car we had in '70, with Bud Moore, and we won a few races that year. We ran three or four and won a couple—finished high in a couple of others. But we didn't have any budget—it wasn't really a Ford program—we didn't run all the races—and so we didn't do too well in the championship."

---

pulled the punches on those." Because the production Boss 302 was a mid-year introduction, they went ahead and omitted the fake air scoops on the 1969½ Boss 302 also, but not on the Boss 429.

So the production Boss 302 was a 100 percent "in-house" assembly. Introduced in mid-model year 1969, it was catalogued as an option for the sports-roof body style (#63), and continued through 1970 with minor changes. For $3720, or about $900 more than the standard sports-roof, the buyer got a Boss 302 with a special high-performance 302, a competition suspension, plus special graphics and accessories. It was a spectacular looking car, with performance to match.

Right out of the box, those Boss 302s could turn 6500 rpm and more, and with better valve springs you could go on up to 8000 rpm. Because such high revs encourage daylight-seeking pistons, Ford installed electronic rev limiters on the 1970 models. They said it protected the engine from over-revving. It also protected Ford from warranty problems, and disconnecting that limiter could void the warranty.

Simply put, the Boss 302 V-8 was a small block Ford of the 260-289-302 series, topped with cylinder heads from the 351 "Cleveland." Those Cleveland heads feature canted valves with huge ports, allowing for a straighter passage of the fuel/air mix in and out of the engine. Hand in hand with the canted valves is a better shaped combustion chamber, sometimes called a "semi-hemi," that gives superior turbulence. On that first '69½ Boss, intakes measured 2.23 inches, massive for such a

---

Dear Mr. Ford,

Remember back in aught-one, before you started making all those cars, before you put America on wheels? You needed some capital, so you got into this big race out at Grosse Point. The idea was to win $1000 and show the people sitting in the stands and reading the newspapers that you were putting together the best car. But, Alexander Winton was the heavy favorite, and nobody allowed you one chance in ten of winning. But you jumped into that primitive racing car with the 550 cubic-inch, two-cylinder engine; and with Spider Huff clinging to the side, balancing that hot rod around the turns, you beat the old pro Winton. The way I read it, the two of you took over 13 minutes to go ten times around that one mile oval track. And when you got out of that car, you flat retired, saying, "Once is enough." Must have been a real spine-tingling ride. Huh, Mr. Ford?

But even though you retired, you built a few more "hot rods." There was old "999" and its near twin, the "Arrow". You knew that the way to sell cars was to give them a real racing image, so they would get the newspaper ink and the applause of the crowd. Race on Sunday, sell on Monday—right Mr. Ford? You were nobody's fool. You got other sports to drive the cars, like old Barney Oldfield, who was one of the guys you met the first race day at Grosse Point.

In June 1903 you started another auto adventure, the Ford Motor Company. You got back to manufacturing, backed out of racing, dropped plans of barnstorming across the country. Your wife Clara was pretty pleased about that too. But you needed some more publicity, and set out to break the world land speed record.

You retrieved the old Arrow from a pile of broken pieces in the Detroit yards of the Pere Marquette Railroad. That was in the warmer days of 1903, the early fall. In January of 1904 you were ready to try for the record, atop the frozen surface of Lake St. Clair. With newspaper people and timers and spectators gathered, and again with ole Spider Huff hugging the sides of the car, you blasted down the ice at near zero temperatures, while that giant, wooden-framed hulk of a car sent gunshot echoes from its 1155 cubic-inch four cylinder. And when the two of you finally came to a stop in a snowbank, narrowly missing the snowbound schooner Garibaldi, you had set a new record: 91.37 mph for the flying mile. Bravo, Mr. Ford!

But I wish you could have been with us when we drove one of your later model cars, this Boss 302 Mustang. Because I had to think of you, and Spider Huff and Barney Oldfield when I got a crack at this baby. I wish you could have been sitting in the car when we tached that 302 up to seven grand! And I know you would have enjoyed watching Jones and Follmer push their racing 302s to 170 on the straights, and take the Trans-Am champion in 1970.

Sincerely,
Jerry Heasley

1.

2.

3.

4.

small volume engine. Of course, it was supposed to flow so much better than the other V-8s of its size. But just think, even the intakes on a 426 Chrysler Hemi measure 2.25 inches! Before deciding on the big canted valve heads, Ford toyed with a "tunnel port" head for the 302 that featured huge "D"-shaped intake ports with the pushrods running in tubes within the ports. Ford decided instead to go with big valves and a more conventional head. At high rpm, those 2.23-inch intakes come on strong, but at low rpm, performance suffers. In 1970, Ford downsized intakes to 2.19-inches, supposedly for a more streetable car.

The rest of the engine was also built extra tough—four-bolt mains (on the center three caps), forged steel crank, forged steel connecting rods, extruded pop-up pistons, dual point ignition, high-rise intake, 780 CFM Holley carb, high pressure oil pump, oil windage baffle, anti-surge baffle (to assure oil pickup under hard acceleration), and a host of other high performance details.

The rear suspension featured staggered shocks and a stabilizer bar. Even though the Boss 302 was a special package, it was more of a regular production unit, without exotic suspension modifications such as lowering the upper control arm—a change common with the earlier GT-350 Shelbys. That would have been too expensive. It was much cheaper to pivot the left shock behind the axle and the right one ahead. This setup really worked to damp out

wheel hop under hard acceleration. Later, in 1970, every Mustang with the competition suspension option had a rear stabilizer bar. And, any 1969 or 1970 Mustang with a 428 and four speed also had staggered rear shocks.

The front spoiler, rear spoiler, "sport-slats," reflective Boss 302 tape stripes, and other black-out trim were developed by Larry Shinoda, design executive of the Special Projects Design Office. They really make the 302 look "boss." The front spoiler was standard, and came delivered in the trunk for dealer installation. The tape striping was also standard, but the rear deck lid wing and the sportslats were optional. In addition, in 1970, the shaker hood scoop, made popular on the 1969 Mach I Mustang with 428CJ, was expanded to include the Boss 302.

Driving Impressions

What's it like to drive a Boss 302? When we first cruised the streets of Borger, Texas, sitting happily in the '70 model pictured on these pages, my first impression was: It feels like I'm riding in a three-quarter-ton pickup! Those springs are super stiff, and rudely jolt vital organs when the Boss bounds over those little drainage channels between intersections. Takeoff from a traffic light is sluggish. The engine sounds like it's about to stall, and then you squirt another gulp of premium through that 780 Holley and you're rolling. It's a chore to drive in stop-and-go traffic.

Along the freeway, with obstructing cars ahead, our Boss danced from lane to lane with the alacrity of a mountain goat. Traction, via those wide oval "60"

specifications

Illustrations by Russell von Sauers, The Graphic Automobile Studio

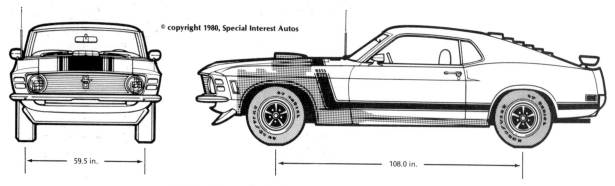

© copyright 1980, Special Interest Autos

59.5 in.

108.0 in.

1970 Ford Mustang Boss 302

Price when new	$3720 (base).
Standard equipment	Boss 302 engine, four-speed transmission with Hurst shifter, competition suspension, dual exhausts, special cooling package, 3.50 non-locking axle, front spoiler, Boss 302 tape identification on front fender (black only), space saver spare, bodyside/hood stripes, black taillamp bezels, black chrome backlite molding and black headlamp castings, color-keyed dual racing mirrors, black hood and rear deck lid and black lower back panel, tachometer, 45-ampere battery, power front disc brakes.
Optional equipment	Sportslats, rear wing spoiler, shaker hood scoop, radio, tilt steering wheel.

ENGINE
Type	90-degree ohv V-8.
Bore and stroke	4.002 x 3.00.
Displacement	302 cu. in.
Max. bhp @ rpm	290 @ 5800.
Max. torque @ rpm	290 @ 4300.
Compression ratio	10.5:1.
Induction system	One four-bbl Holley.
Exhaust system	Dual, two passage reverse flow mufflers, one lateral reverse flow muffler.
Electrical system	12-volt battery, coil.

CLUTCH
Type	Semi-centrifugal, single disc, dry plate.
Disc diameter	10.4-in.
Actuation	Mechanical via foot pedal.

TRANSMISSION
Type		Manual, four-speed, synchronized in forward gears, Hurst floor shifter.
Ratios:	1st	2.78 (2.32 optional).
	2nd	1.93 (1.69 optional).
	3rd	1.36 (1.29 optional).
	4th	1.00 (1.00 optional).
	Rev	2.78 (2.32 optional).

DIFFERENTIAL
Type	Rear-conventional, 9.0-in. ring gear.
Ratio	3.50:1, optional 3.50, 3.91 "Traction-Lok" and 4.30 "Detroit Locker."
Drive axles	Semi floating, straddle mounted pinion.

STEERING
Type	Recirculating ball and nut with power assist (manual is standard).
Turns lock to lock	3.74.
Ratio	16:1 (gear), 20.32:1 (overall).
Turn circle	37.6 feet (curb to curb).

BRAKES
Type	Caliper disc (front), duo servo drums (rear). Power.
Drum diameter	11.3-in. dia. front rotor and 10.0-in. rear drum.
Total lining area	505.8 sq. in.

CHASSIS AND BODY
Frame	Unitized.
Body construction	Steel.
Body style	Two-door fastback coupe.

SUSPENSION
Front	Independent, single lateral arm with drag strut, ball joints, coil springs and shock absorbers mounted over upper arm.
Rear	Hotchkiss drive design, semi-elliptical steel springs, staggered shock absorbers.
Tires	F60 x 15, belted four-plys (two fiberglass, two polyester) "Goodyear Polyglass GT."
Wheels	15 x 7 stamped steel.

WEIGHTS AND MEASURES
Wheelbase	108.0 in.
Overall length	187.4 in.
Overall height	50.4 in.
Overall width	71.8 in.
Front tread	59.5 in.
Rear tread	59.5 in.
Ground clearance	4.1 in. at front spoiler
Curb weight	3122 lbs.

CAPACITIES
Crankcase	5.0 qt.
Cooling system	13.5 qt.
Fuel tank	22.0 gal.

FUEL CONSUMPTION
Best	12-14 mpg.
Average	10-12 mpg.

Marque Club Address
Mustang Owner's Club
2829 Cagua Dr. NE
Albuquerque, NM 87110

Shelby Owners of America
2851 So. Mead
Wichita, KS 67216

Parnelli Jones, shown here, along with George Follmer campaigned Bud Moore-prepared Boss 302s in SCCA Trans-Am Championship racing with great success.

photo courtesy SCCA

series radials on this car is spectacular, and you feel their bite right through the seat of your pants! Then, after you Trans-Am your way through traffic pretending you're Parnelli Jones, you tach that engine up there to five or six grand, and it's a real thrill. There's no hesitation or bogging once that fastback is rolling. Power comes on so very strongly that when you let off the gas pedal it feels as though you've stomped on the brakes. And once you get the hang of it, you can really slap that Hurst T-Handle finger-grip shifter through those gears.

Amazingly, the Boss on these pages was so stock, so original, it still had the rev limiter intact. Back in 1969, having a governor on your engine was akin to carrying your American history teacher in the back seat while you went through the quarter-mile. The limiter restricted engine speed to around 6000 rpm. Tuned right, these engines will go up to 7000 rpm without the limiter, and this writer has driven several cars with that rev range.

Ford Motor Co.

1.

2.

1. '69 Boss differs from '70 mostly in front end design. 2. Big, round white-on-black instruments for easy reading. 3. Dual exhaust system aided breathing on high-revving 302. 4. Action with a Shelby Racing Boss 302 during a Trans-Am battle. 5. There's nothing subtle about the 302's aggressive appearance, and bright colors added to their visual excitement.

3.

photo courtesy SCCA

4.

5.

With a sharp Boss 302, rolling along in traffic, there's a conceited feeling that engulfs you; in fact, it's virtually a sensual feeling. It's part of the whole experience of owning, driving or riding in this wild-looking super car and helps give the Boss its charisma today. The feeling stems from the Boss name itself, the spoilers front and rear, the high performance engine, the classic, crouched muscle car stance, the sportslats that in profile look like the raised hairs on the back of a bowed cat's back, and numerous other details. And, if anyone asks a question about the car—say one of those teenagers driving a Trans-Am Firebird—you can hit him with all manner of technical talk, from canted

valves, to downward thrust of the rear spoiler and how it keeps you on the road at 140, to how the 1970 Boss beat everything in Trans-Am in 1970—and on, and on. A fully decked out Boss is hard to upstage. ☙

Above: Rev Limited was installed on '70 Bosses. Left: You don't have to own an oil well to run a Boss, but with its appetite for premium fuel, it helps.

Who Named It "Boss"?

It was Larry Shinoda who came up with the idea to call the new high-performance Mustang series by the name "Boss." Larry explained to us that the "product planning and marketing people had some screwy names that I didn't much care for. One of them was 'SR-2,' which was supposed to stand for 'Sedan Racing, Group 2'." But Larry had a better name in mind. He told them that Boss 302 "would probably make more sense," and then he mentioned that they could "call the larger engine job the Boss 429." In retrospect, it was a great system for naming these high-performance Mustangs, and when the longer, lower, wider 1971 models came along, there was a Boss 351 Mustang.

However, Larry said that back in 1968, "there was a pretty big hassle about it, because they had already picked the SR-2 name." But when the

Boss name was put before Bunkie Knudsen and Henry Ford II, Shinoda explained to us that, "they actually thought it had a good sound." According to Shinoda, both men liked the name over the others, although it was Henry who actually selected it.

It has been a successful name, helping promote the car among today's collectors, but back in 1969 and 1970, it was a word that had passed its prime. Remember the movie *American Graffiti*? Remember the girl who mentioned the "boss" car? Well, the word "boss" has been applied to cars for years, at least clear back to the fifties. And up until about 1965, it was still very popular. I listened to some tapes of a Los Angeles radio station disc jockey that were made in 1965, and it seemed like every other word was "boss." Boss jocks played boss records to teenagers in their

boss cars driving around Boss Angeles. There was even a local contest in which the winner got a new Mustang—a "boss" Mustang, of course.

Obviously, boss was a synonym for the leader, the one in command—the boss! A boss car could blow the doors off any other machine in town. Then it was boss.

By 1969 and 1970, however, the word had been over-used, and had really died out from the vernacular of the young. *Car and Driver*, reporting on the "slow burn" in the youth market, in 1969, recorded one young girl's comments, who said that "boss" went out with "bitchin" and "stoked."

Even so, that oily-shirted speed shop crowd liked the name, and the car. Detroit might have been five years late tagging a car Boss, but they put it on a winner.

Season after season of Trans-Am wins with specially prepared Mustangs taught us how to set up Boss 302.

'70 Boss 302–Son of Trans-Am.

The Mustang Boss 302 is what comes from winning Trans-Am races year after year. It's designed to go quick and hang tight. The standard specs sound like a $9,000 European sports job instead of a reasonably priced, reliable American pony car. Boss 302 comes in just one body style—the wind-splitting SportsRoof shape. The engine is Ford's high output 302 CID 4V V-8, with new cylinder heads to permit canting the valves for better gas flow and larger diameter. That's what gives you a big 290 horsepower from a small, lightweight 302 CID engine.

Choose either close or wide ratios on Boss 302's buttersmooth, fully synchronized 4-speed. We've made it an even quicker box by adding a T-Handle Hurst Shifter®.

Brakes are power boosted, ventilated floating-caliper front discs. When we tell you the suspension is competition type with staggered rear shocks to combat rear wheel hop on takeoff, don't take our word for it, give it a try. We glue the Boss to the road on 15-inch wheels shod with F60-15 superwide fiberglass belted, bias ply tires. All this leaves you little to option but the fun things—like Magnum 500 chrome wheels, and those great Sport Slats for the tinted backlite. That's Boss 302. Your only problem . . . deciding whether to drive it or "Trans-Am" it.

For the full story on all the performance Fords for 1970, visit your Ford Dealer, and get our big 16-page 1970 Performance Digest. Or write to:

FORD PERFORMANCE DIGEST, Dept. RT-7, P.O. Box 747, Dearborn, Michigan 48121.

MUSTANG Ford

Paint a number on your Boss 302, put a big gas tank in it, and call yourself Parnelli Jones.

1970 FORD MUSTANG MACH 1 COBRA JET

by John F. Katz
photos by Roy Query

"BACK then we did some crazy things."

Ken Spencer spent the late sixties as a Ford design executive, working under studio director Joe Oros. One of the crazier things he and his colleagues did was to design a functional air scoop that bolted down to the top of the engine air cleaner and poked up through a hole in the front hood. "You should have heard the screams in the design studio," he recalled, with obvious relish. "The engineers went nuts...you know, they never would allow us to stick anything out through the hood, because when the engine rocks when you accelerate, it hits things."

Sure, the engineers screamed. But then they scurried back to their slide rules and figured out how to make it happen. There was still time for a little craziness, in the days before safety and emissions and other pesky social responsibilities loomed too large in the automakers' priorities. Even as the car on these pages was being built, however, that time was coming to an end. The 1970 Mustang was the last of the breed to have descended directly from the spectacularly successful 1964½ original. It was also the very last Mustang to offer the mighty 428 Cobra Jet V-8, itself the last of a line of engines that began with the Thunderbird 352 in 1958 and included the NASCAR-bred, Le Mans-winning 427. 1971 would bring a new

Originally published in Special Interest Autos #122, Mar.-Apr. 1991

Driving Impressions

by Roy D. Query and John F. Katz

We remember the Mach 1 Mustang as a kind of Hot Wheels car for older kids — all scoops and stripes pasted over some of the sixties' most awful colors, as busy and overstated as a study-hall doodle. Somehow, though, Rick Parker's is different. Maybe it's the unusual black-on-black color scheme that lends Rick's car a certain cohesion and integrity that's just not possible in Medium Lime Metallic.

Inside, the massive dash and large-diameter steering wheel sit too close relative to the pedals; this would be an awfully awkward car for a short person to drive. But the seats offer decent comfort, and Rick, who stands just six feet tall, says that the car fits him fine.

The starter motor coughs once before the engine lights up and then settles down to a busy, whirring, almost liquid rumble. The shaker hood dances its restless mambo, immediately commanding the driver's attention. The sensitive clutch works like a toggle switch; either it's in or it's out, with precious little in between.

With no power assist to numb the steering, the wheel feeds back every sharp corner of the gravel in the drive. We pull onto the pavement and take her once through the gears, gently, limiting our shifts to 3,500 rpm: Snort, snort, howwwwl! howwwwl! howwwwl! Once above idle, the big mill makes more rush than rumble, a sound that somehow recalls the starship

Enterprise (old generation) hurtling past Warp 9. The nylon bias-ply tires haven't quite reached operating temperature, and they deliver a firm bumpity-bump to the seat of our pants. And then there's that hood scoop, twitching nervously between shifts, always in the corner of our vision.

The "competition" suspension delivers as rough a ride as we expected, and the hood shakes and rattles in true vintage Detroit fashion. The seats must soak up some of the harshness, because we can *hear* the suspension working over the few bumps we don't *feel*. Patched-up chuckholes kick back through the steering wheel. But the power front disc brakes work surprisingly well for their age and era — and so does the heater.

The twisty service road behind the Port Columbus airport offers a number of challenging off-camber curves. Unfortunately, most of the curves offer telephone poles just beyond the apex. Despite its direct feel, the Mustang's steering is neither light nor quick, and with nearly 60 percent of the car's weight on its front wheels, it shouldn't surprise anyone that this old Detroiter isn't particularly interested in deviating from a straight line. Not that it pushes real hard, but once in a turn we definitely feel as though the front end is going to slip out from underneath us before the rear end comes around. Of course, we're sure we could break the back

tires loose with a generous stab of power — but those telephone poles look pretty sturdy.

Clearly, the Mach 1 does its best work in a straight line. The accelerator is sensitive; our right foot barely toes the pedal and the big 428 stuffs us a little deeper into the high-back vinyl seat. There's a sharp rasp from the motor at 4,000 rpm that wasn't there below 3,500. We slow down to let the traffic pull ahead of us, then, coasting at 2,000 rpm in first gear, we punch it — hard. The engine rushes for the red zone with a hurricane howl. Did the tires slip? They didn't make any noise, and we don't see any tire smoke, but then it's pretty windy, too, so it's hard to tell. Into second at 3,000 rpm, we punch it again, bringing down a maelstrom of wind and engine and road noise. Two black marks, maybe 40 feet long, appear in the rear-view mirror. But there is still no tire noise and no fishtailing — just two straight black lines stretched out behind us.

Rick offers to show us how it's done. He has no trouble wagging the tail and coaxing a squeal from the rear tires on a first-second upshift before a late-model Grand Am meanders into our lane. Passing the errant Pontiac, Rick burns rubber in the bottom three gears. Says he could do it in fourth, too, by side-stepping the clutch, but he doesn't want to treat his car that way. We can't say we blame him.

MUSTANG

decade, a new Mustang, and, to an extent, a new era.

"The 428 was...a seven-liter engine that could be made at high volume," explained Bill Barr, the Ford engineer who headed the Cobra Jet project, "as opposed to the 427, which was more high-bred, special purpose." Less bore and more stroke not only endowed the 428 with more low-end torque than its famous ancestor, but simplified machining as well. The first 428s appeared in 1966 in Ford's police interceptors and as an option for the Galaxie XL and Thunderbird.

Ford built a few 427 Mustangs early in the '68 model year, but the company soon realized that a massaged and modified 428 could compete more cost-effectively against Chevrolet's new 396 Camaro. then someone suggested that the Cobra name could be milked for some more mileage. "It was really a very simple project," Barr recalled. "We took a cam we were using in the 390 GT, [and] took what amounted to the 428 police interceptor intake manifold — which happened to be aluminum, but for the Cobra Jet in order to save money we made it out of iron." High-performance heads from the old 427 and an upgraded carburetor — from 600 to 735 cfm — completed the package. The Cobra Jet found its way onto the Mustang GT option sheet midway through 1968, bowing officially on April 1 of that year. Barr quipped that the hulking engine fit into the smallish Mustang only because the assembly-line workers didn't know that it couldn't possibly.

Nonetheless, Barr was present to watch one of those blissfully unin-

Illustrations by Russell von Sauers, The Graphic Automobile Studio

specifications

58.5 in.

108.0 in.

1970 Ford Mustang Mach 1 Cobra Jet

Price	$3,271
Standard equipment on Mach 1 includes	351 c.i.d., 250 hp V-8; electric clock; dual color-keyed racing mirrors; deluxe Decor Group interior; deluxe Rim-Blow steering wheel; competition suspension
Options on dR car	428 c.i.d., 335 hp Cobra Jet with Ram Air, $376; 4-speed transmission, $205; Traction-Lok rear end, $43; power front disc brakes, $65; AM radio, $61; tachometer and trip odometer, $54; quick-ratio steering, $16; fold-down rear seat, $97
Total price	$4,188

ENGINE
Type	90-degree V-8
Bore x stroke	4.13" x 3.98"
Displacement	428 cu. in.
Compression ratio	10.6:1
Bhp (gross) @ rpm	335 @ 5,200
Torque @ rpm	440 @ 3,400
Taxable hp	54.6
Valve gear	ohv
Valve lifters	Hydraulic
Main bearings	5
Induction system	1 Holley R-4513 4-bbl. carburetor with vacuum secondaries, mechanical pump
Lubrication system	Full pressure
Exhaust system	Dual
Electrical system	12-volt

TRANSMISSION
Type	4-speed manual
Ratios: 1st	2.32:1
2nd	1.69:1
3rd	1.29:1
4th	1.00:1
Reverse	2.32:1

DIFFERENTIAL
Type	Traction-Lok limited slip
Final drive	3.50:1

STEERING
Type	Recirculating ball
Turns lock-to-lock	3.7
Ratios	16.1:1 (gear); 20.3:1 (overall)
Turning circle	37' 5" curb/curb

BRAKES
System	4-wheel hydraulic, vacuum assisted
Type/diameter	11.3" vented disc (front); 10.0" drum (rear)
Total swept area	341 sq. in.

CONSTRUCTION
Type	Unitized
Body construction	All steel
Body style	2-door hardtop coupe

SUSPENSION
Front	Independent, coil springs, ball joints, upper wishbones, single lower arms with drag struts, anti-roll bar
Rear	Live axle, semi-elliptic springs, anti-roll bar

Shock absorbers	Tubular hydraulic, staggered in rear
Wheels	14x6" pressed steel disc
Tires	Goodyear F70-14

WEIGHTS AND MEASURES
Wheelbase	108.0"
Overall length	187.4"
Overall width	71.3"
Overall height	51.2"
Front track	58.5"
Rear track	58.5"
Ground clearance	6.1"
Curb weight	3,647 lb.

CAPACITIES
Crankcase	5.0 qt.
Transmission	1.0 qt.
Cooling system	20.0 qt.
Fuel tank	20.0 gal.

CALCULATED DATA
Bhp/c.i.d.	0.78
Lb./bhp	10.9*
Lb./c.i.d.	8.5*
P.S.I. (brakes)	10.7*

PRODUCTION
Total 1970 Mustang	190,727
Total 1970 Mach 1	40,970
Total '70 Mustang Cobra Jet	2,671
Total '70 Mach 1 Cobra Jet	N/a

*estimated weight

*Facing page, top: Ribbed aluminum rocker panels were part of '70 Mach I's dress-up trim. **Center:** Goodyear Polyglas tires were also stock equipment. **Bottom:** For 1970, Mustangs returned to dual head-lamps from the quads used in '69. **This page:** Mach I has a purposeful yet graceful profile which bristles with promises of power.*

Left: While '70 Boss 302 used a matte black lower panel, the Mach I uses this honeycomb trim. *Right:* Dual exhausts are standard, of course.

MUSTANG

Meet The New Boss

The 428 Cobra Jet was neither the largest nor theoretically the most powerful engine offered in the '69-70 Mustang. That distinction belonged to the very-limited-production Boss 429, a street-tuned version of Ford's hemi-head NASCAR powerplant. Despite the Boss's competition pedigree, however, enthusiasts today generally remember it as a high-strung dud, impressive on paper but useless on the street.

Could the Cobra Jet actually outrun the Boss? The only contemporary road tests we found pit an option-laden, automatic-transmission Cobra Jet against a lowered and blueprinted B/Stock Boss 429 equipped with drag slicks and bleach dispensers. (We ferreted out a test of the Plymouth Hemi-'Cuda, too, as an exotic-engine benchmark.) We aren't about to pretend that the resulting table proves anything, except, perhaps, that the Boss 429 could turn a pretty mean quarter mile with just a minimum of modification.

Folks who know both cars well, however, invariably prefer the Cobra Jet. "It will blow the doors off [a 429]," says Parker, who should know. "In stock trim, there's no comparison.... Not only does the Cobra Jet deliver more torque sooner, it even gets the power to the pavement more effectively — despite its smaller, F70-14 tires."

Larry Shinoda, who designed the graphics for the Boss 429, as well as the far more

successful small-block Boss 302, once owned a Boss 302 with a blueprinted 428 Cobra Jet lurking inside. "It would actually outrun a Boss 429 hands down," he told us. He remembers drag racing against a Boss 429 at the Dearborn test track: "I had the air conditioner going and the stereo playing and I just flat blew him away. And [my car] was an automatic, not a four-speed. And they had the clock set up and everything, and with all that I cut a 14.50, at 107, and the fastest that Boss 429 would run was 99 at 15.01."

Out of the box, the Boss arrived with too little carburetor or cam to take advantage of its enormous, free-breathing heads. But the boss engine's problems ran deeper than that. Originally conceived for longevity and smooth cruising in full-sized luxury cars, the 429 V-8 carried three-inch mains and proportionately enormous rods and rod bearings. The race-bred Boss simply lacked the low-rpm grunt needed to overcome the rotating inertia of that kind of machinery.

"You could wind it up to 7,000 rpm and run there all day," said Barr — fine for running 500 high-speed miles on NASCAR's banked ovals, but hardly a useful advantage on a drag strip. "The advantage the 428 had was that at 2,000 rpm, it was pulling pretty good power.... As long as you got it up to 10 mph...you [could] squeeze on it and it would chug away. In a 429, you just couldn't do that."

formed workers drive the first Cobra-Jet Mustang off the old Dearborn line, where the ancient wood-block floor was "covered with 40 years of grease and tire and dum-dum and oil.... The first one that came off...happened to be a four-speed top-loader, and...he just spun his way all across the area." Then they put the car on the rollers for testing: "This guy took off and flat-pedaled this 428.... He didn't stop until he ran it up well over 100 mph on the indicator.... The guy turned around, [and] he had [such] a grin, it was fortunate the top of his head didn't fall off."

Yeah, they did some crazy things back then.

1969 brought little mechanical change to the Mustang, but all-new sheet metal gave Ford's aging pony a racier, more muscular look. The new "Mach 1" model, named for the radically chopped and lowered Mustang show car that Ford had first displayed late in 1966, featured a stiffer "competition" suspension and a more deluxe interior than its plainer stablemates.

The "shaker" hood scoop appeared that year as well, as standard equipment on the Ram-Air Cobra Jet (428CJ-R for short) and as an option on selected other Mustang V-8s. A predetermined drop in manifold pressure opened a flapper valve between the scoop and the air cleaner, force-feeding cold air to the engine just when it needed it the most. Ever wary of trinkets and tomfoolery, the staff of *Car and Driver* tested a new Mach 1 CJ-R in November 1968 — with and without its scoop taped shut — and discovered, to their surprise and delight, that the pot-metal snorkel actually cut the Mustang's quarter-mile time by 0.2 seconds while boosting its trap speed two mph.

"If that's true," argued Spencer, "it was just pure luck.... I'm not sure the

Comparative Specifications:	428 Cobra Jet	Boss 429
Displacement, c.i.	428	429
Bore x stroke, in.	4.13x3.98	4.36x3.59
Compression ratio	10.6:1	10.5:1
Carburetion, cfm	735	735
Inlet valve diameter, in.	2.097	2.285
Exhaust valve diameter, in.	1.665	1.905
Lifters	Hydraulic	Mechanical
Advertised bhp @ rpm	335 @ 5,200	375 @ 5,200
Advertised torque @ rpm, lb./ft.	440 @ 3,400	450 @ 3,400

Performance	Mach 1 CJ*	Boss 429**	Hemi-Cuda***
Weight of test car, lb.	3,607	3,400	3,880
Weight distribution, f/r	59/41	56/44	N/a
Transmission	3-spd. auto.	4-spd. manual	3-spd. auto
Final drive	3.91:1	4.56:1	3.55:1
Tire size	F70-14	7" slick	F60-15
0-30, sec.	2.1	2.2	2.8
0-60, sec.	5.7	5.3	5.8
¼ mile, sec. @ mph	14.3 @ 100	12.3 @ 112	14.0 @ 102

* *Car and Driver*, November 1968
** *Motor Trend*, April 1970 (test car had stock blueprinted engine, but its chassis was mildly modified for drag racing)
*** *Motor Trend*, May 1970

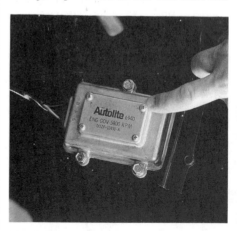

Rev limiter helps prevent daylight-seeking pistons.

darn thing worked." Who cared, though, as long as it looked neat on the street?

Not much changed for '70, really. Base Mustangs shed some vents and emblems for a cleaner look, largely at the behest of new Ford president Semon E. "Bunkie" Knudsen. "He didn't like fake scoops and things that didn't do anything," recalled Gale Halderman, a 35-year veteran of Ford Design. "He was trying to get rid of that kind of stuff." Despite Bunkie's best efforts, however, the '70 Mach 1 actually collected a bit more gingerbread, including heavy-looking ribbed aluminum rocker panels, grille-mounted driving lamps, and a bogus honeycomb grille between the taillamps. Quick-ratio steering became available as an option, a genuine Hurst shifter replaced the somewhat flimsy linkage used previously on four-speed models, and all Mustangs with competition suspension benefited from a rear anti-roll bar: ½-inch on 351s and ⅝-inch on 428s.

Our featured 1970 Mach 1 Cobra Jet belongs to Rick Parker of Columbus, Ohio, a self-described "Ford nut" whose garage has also housed several Boss 302s, three Boss 429s (his white '69 Boss 429 appeared on the cover of *SIA* #75), plus a number of Shelby Mustangs and Panteras. He drag raced Boss 302s for six years, and currently owns a 1963 Galaxie convertible with a 427 and a four-speed.

Top: Shaker hood scoop was a stock item on Cobra Jet engines. **Above:** *driveReport car's trim tag confirms its originality and correctness.* **Below:** *Spare tire takes up a goodly amount of the limited trunk space.*

MUSTANG

Above: *High-back buckets offer plenty of style but little grip during ambitious cornering.* **Right:** *Fold-down back seat is great for little kids, not so hot for full-sized folks.*

Rick's Mustang was originally sold through C&C Motors in Horsham, Pennsylvania. The date on the invoice reads September 9, 1969 — only six days after the '70 models debuted. Somehow, the car made its way to Florida — a conspicuously unsuitable environment for a black-on-black automobile with no air conditioning — where a neighbor of Rick's bought it in 1977 for $700. Rick's neighbor towed the Mustang home to Columbus, where a worn-out lifter lured him into replacing the original engine. The car didn't run after that; as Rick put it, "mechanically inclined he wasn't.... Luckily, he kept 99 percent of all the parts for this car. This car still has the original exhaust system on it.... It still has the original Ford shock absorbers on it. It's just incredible how original it really is." With no rust to remove, and virtually no missing parts to hunt down, Rick was able to reassemble the car in just six months. He did have it repainted its original Raven Black with matte black stripes.

Ford unveiled an all-new and significantly larger Mustang for 1971 — large enough, in fact, for a wedge-head edition of Ford's newest seven-liter power-

When Mach I is set up to win 8000 miles of rallying in stock trim, it's got to be a great car to get across town in.

Mach 1–pronounced Mach Won!

Winning is a habit with Mach 1. The latest triumph is the top rally award a car can win on this continent—the SCCA Manufacturer's Rally Championship for 1969. To win it you've got to run over 8,000 miles of rallies on all kinds of roads in all kinds of weather and finish every stage with split-second precision. That means sprinting acceleration; hanging tight when you corner, brakes that won't quit and power to ram your way through snow-clogged mountain passes. Mach 1 wins rally after rally because Mach 1's got what it takes: a balanced wide-tread chassis and sports-car design suspension, with front and rear stabilizer bars, extra-heavy-duty springs, shocks, and wide-rim wheels.

Power is what you get with any of Mach's great V-8's—a 351 2V is standard. Your first option is the brand-new free-breathing 351 4V Cleveland engine with canted valve heads and 300 horsepower that turns on

right now. From there on you option the 428 Cobra V-8 and its partner in power, the Cobra Jet Ram-Air. That's the one with the functional "Shaker" that pops up through the hood to ram cool air.

For '70 the Mach 1 looks as good as it goes. There's a unique black grille with special sports lamps, matte black hood, aluminum rocker panels, high-back buckets, full instrumentation, woodtoned panel and console, electric clock, and more. Get yourself a Mach 1 and really "shake up" the troops.

See your Ford Dealer for a free copy of the 1970 Performance Buyer's Digest or write to:

FORD PERFORMANCE DIGEST, Dept. MT-22, Box 747, Dearborn, Michigan 48121.

MUSTANG *Ford*

After 8000 miles of gruelling competition the Mustang team wrapped up the Manufacturer's Rally Championship for 1969.

plant, the gargantuan 429. (Ford had shoehorned a hemi-head 429 into a limited number of '69-70 "Boss 429" Mustangs only by extensively customizing the engine bay and front suspension.) The now-obsolete 428 disappeared as a Mustang option — as would the 429 after only one model year. Within three years, Ford had transferred the noble Mustang name to a rebodied Pinto with V-6 power.

The time for doing crazy things was over. □

Acknowledgements and Bibliography

John A. Gunnel (editor), Standard Catalog of American Cars 1946-1975; *Richard M. Langworth and Graham Robson,* Complete Book of Collectible Cars 1940-1980; *Peter Sessler,* Mustang Red Book: Early 1965-90; *A.B. Shuman,* "All the King's Horses," *Motor Trend, April 1970; Gary L. Witzenburg,* Mustang: The Complete History of America's Pioneer Ponycar; *"428 Mustang Mach I,"* Car and Driver, *November 1968.*

Thanks to Bill Barr, Gale Halderman, Linda Lee, and Paul Preuss of the Ford Motor Company; Kim M. Miller of the AACA Library and Research Center; Henry Siegle; Larry Shinoda; Ken Spencer; and of course our special thanks to Rick Parker.

Above: The only external clue to the engine's potential is this script on each side of the hood scoop. Left: Fold-down seat compensates for skimpy trunk space. Below: With Cobra Jet equipment, the Mach I was far more Mustang than the average commuter needed.

Mustang Clubs & Specialists

For a complete list of all regional Mustang clubs and national clubs' chapters, visit **Car Club Central** at **www.hemmings.com**. With nearly 10,000 car clubs listed, it's the largest car club site in the world! Not wired? For the most up-to-date information, consult the latest issue of *Hemmings Motor News* and or *Hemmings' Collector Car Almanac*. Call toll free, 1-800-CAR-HERE, Ext. 550.

MUSTANG CLUBS

Aloha Mustang and Shelby Club of Hawaii
Mr. Mumper
P.O. Box 6216
Honolulu, HI 96818
808-261-4090

Boss 302 Registry
Randy Ream
1817 Janet Ave.
Lebanon, PA 17082

Boss 351 Registry
Jerry Richard
P.O. Box 26644
Jacksonville, FL 32218

Boss 429 Owner's Directory
Steve Strange
P.O. Box 8035
Spokane, WA 99203
509-448-0252

Ford T-5 Owner's Registry
Gary Hansen
P.O. Box 808 L-130
Livermore, CA 94550
415-422-4073

428 Cobra Jet Registry
Gary Pientraniec
6890 Plainfield
Dearborn, MI 48127
313-274-1513

GT/CS California Special Registry
Paul M. Newitt
P.O. Box 2013
El Macero, CA 95618

Metuchen-Built '71 Mustang Registry
1530 11th St., P.O. Box 103
Fennimore, WI 53809

Mustang Club of America
3588 Hwy. 138, Suite 365
Stockbridge, GA 30281
770-477-1965
www.mustang.org

Mustang Owner's Club International
Paul MacLaughlin
2720 Tennessee N.E.
Albuquerque, NM 87110
505-296-2254

Mustang Road Race Registry
Ed Lutke
28763 Greening
Farmington Hills, MI 48018-4705

Mustang 63D Registry
5425 Rawlings St.
Flower Mound, TX 75028

Mustangs Across America
Sam Haymart
P.O. Box 4131
Citrus Heights, CA 95611-4131

Mustang II, Pinto, And Pinto Cruiser Wagon Owner's Club & Registry
212 Providence Rd., Suite 206
Charlotte, NC 28207

National Mustang Association
9200 Foxcroft Ave.
Clinton, MD 20735

Third-Generation National Registry
Stew Jones
923 Raleigh Rd.
Palm Bay, FL 32909
407-984-1125

1965-66 Mustang Coupe Registry
Tony Castelletti
735 Delaware Rd., #165
Buffalo, NY 14223

1965-1969 GT Registry
16830 Stahelin
Detroit, MI 48219

1966 Sprint 200/Early Six Registry
27534 140th St. S.E.
Kent, WA 98042

1968 Gold Nugget Special Registry
Willam R. O'Gorman
P.O. Box 301
Cortland, NY 13045

1966, '67, '68 High Country Special Registry
Bob Teets
6874 Benton Court
Arvada, CO 80003
303-424-3866

1967 K-Code Mustang Registry
608-526-6619

1968 Mustang Convertible Registry
838 Bewrtha Ave.
Akron, OH 44306

1968 "S" Code Registry
403 N. Gladstone Ave.
Indianapolis, IN 46201

1968 V-8 Sprint Registry
23 Mount Dr.
Holmdel, NJ 07733

1968 X-Code Mustang Registry
583 Ranchero Rd., Suite 1
Belle Glade, FL 33430

1968½-1970 428 Cobra Jet Convertible Registry
Rt. 1 Box 107B
Winchester, IN 47394

1968½ 428 Cobra Jet Registry
Chris Teeling or Claude LaForest
860-745-5394 or 819-333-5732

1969-70 Shelby Red Interior Registry
613 Dahlia Way
Acworth, GA 30102

1970 Mustang Grabber Sportsroof Registry
Harold C. Jankowiak
2715 Berkshire Dr.
Troy, MI 48083-2604
810-689-9320

1971 429 Mustang Registry
Marvin Scotchorn
6250 Germantown Pike
Dayton, OH 45418

1971-73 Mustang High Performance Coupe Registry
P.O. Box 4233
Cary, NC 27519

1972 Sprint Convertible Registry
1548 Greenwood Cemetery Rd.
Danville, IL 61832

1972 Sprint Registry
Rick Ducher
P.O. Box 2394
Cody, WY 82414

1972 351 H.O. Mustang Registry
9403 Warwick Ave.
Norfolk, VA 23503

1974-78 Mustang II Registry
19964 Fox St.
Redford, MI 48240

1978 King Cobra Registry
P.O. Box 88
Carver, MN 55315-0088
612-448-2931

Performance Ford Club of America
13155 U.S. Route 23
Ashville, OH 43103-0032

Playboy Pink Registry
Jason D. Sellers
P.O. Box 1302
Topeka, KS 66601

Shelby American Automobile Club
Rick Kopec
P.O. Box 788
Sharon, CT 06069
860-364-0449

Shelby Owners of America Inc.
Jim Mollenkamp
P.O. Box 454
Arnold, KS 67515

Special Order Paint Registry
Tony Popish
456 Via de Leon
Placentia, CCA 92870
714-996-2340

Twister Special Registry
7520 N.W. Rochester Route
Topeka, KS 66617

289 Hi-Po "K" Code Registry
3603 W. Congress #229B
Lafayette, LA 70506

United Ford Owners
P.O. Box 32419
Columbus, OH 43232

Vintage Mustang Owner's Association
P.O. Box 5772
San Jose, CA 95150-5772

MUSTANG PARTS SUPPLIERS

Auto Krafters
P.O. Box 8HMMU
Broadway, VA 22815
540-896-5910
New body and trim parts

CT Mustang II
P.O. Box 407
Stratford, CT 06615
203-377-4795
New body and trim parts

Glazier's Mustang Barn
531 Wambold Rd.
Souderton, PA 18964
800-523-6708
New body and mechanical parts

K.A.R. Auto Group
1166 Cleveland Ave.
Columbus, OH 43201
800-341-5949
New body and mechanical parts

Larry's Thunderbird & Mustang Parts, Inc.
511 S. Raymond Ave.
Fullerton, CA 92831
714-871-6432
New body and mechanical parts

MAC's Antique Auto Parts
1051 Lincoln Ave.
Lockport, NY
800-777-0948
New mechanical and trim parts

Mostly Mustangs Inc.
55 Alling St.
Hamden, CT 06517
203-562-4891
Restoration parts and services

Mustangs & More
2065 Sperry Ave., No. C
Ventura, CA 93003
805-642-0887
Restoration parts and services

Mustang Parts of Oklahoma
8801 S. Interstate 35
Oklahoma City, OK 73149-3080
405-631-1400
New body and mechanical parts

Mustangs Unlimited
185 Adams St.
Manchester, CT 06040
800-243-7278
New body and mechanical parts

National Parts Depot
3101 SW 40th Blvd.
Gainesville, FL 32608
352-378-9000
New body and mechanical parts

New England Mustang
P.O. Box 600
Easton, CT 06612
800-242-2314
New body and mechanical parts

Tony Branda Mustang & Shelby
1434 E. Pleasant Valley Blvd.
Altoona, PA 16602
800-458-3477
New body and mechanical parts

MUSTANG SPECIALISTS

Bill Herndon's Pony Warehouse
20028 Cinnabar Dr.
Gaithersburg, MD 20879
301-977-0309
Steering wheel sales and reconditioning

BCD Preservations Inc.
5540 Milford-Harrington HWY.
Harrington, DE 19952
302-398-4014
Restoration parts and service

Classic Auto Air Mfg. Co.
2020 West Kennedy Blvd.,
Tampa, FL 33606
813-251-4994
Air conditioning

Classic Tube
80 Rotech Dr.
Lancaster, NY 14086
800-882-3711
Reproduction brake and fuel lines

Convertible Service
5126-H Walnut Grove Ave.
San Gabriel, CA 91776
626-285-2255
Convertible parts

Dan Williams Toploader Transmissions
206 East Dogwood Dr.
Franklin, NC 28734
828-524-9085
Transmission sales, service, parts

Fitzgerald Automotive Showcase
New Hampshire
603-524-2951
Shelby Mustang restorations

Hydro-E-Lectric
5475 Williamsburg Dr., Unit 8
Punta Gorda, FL 33982
800-343-4261
Convertible parts

Metro
11610 Jay St. P.O. Box 48130
Minneapolis, MN 55448
800-878-2237
Rubber weatherstripping

Phoenix Graphix
5861 S. Kyrene Rd., Suite 10
Tempe, AZ 85283
800-941-4550
Decals and stripes

Pony and Corral
7315 Livingston Rd.
Oxon Hill, MD 20745
301-839-6666
Data plates and trim parts

The Right Stuff
5093 Westerville Rd.
Columbus, OH 43231
800-405-2000
Reproduction brake and fuel lines

SMS AUTO FABRICS
2325 SE 10th Ave.
Portland, OR 97214
503-234-1175
New door panels/upholstery

Specialty Wheels, Ltd.
34566 S.E. Gunderson Rd.
Sandy, OR 97055
503-668-4793
Reproduction wheels, wheel restoration

Engines 1964 ½-1978

Year	Cylinders	Displacement	Bore x Stroke	Output (Gross HP)
1964½	I-6	170-cu.in.	3.50 x 2.94 in.	101
1964½	I-6	200-cu.in.	3.68 x 3.13 in.	116
1964½	V-8	260-cu.in.	3.80 x 2.87 in.	164
1964½	V-8	289-cu.in.	4.00 x 2.87 in.	210
1965	I-6	200-cu.in.	3.68 x 3.13 in.	120
1965	V-8	289-cu.in.	4.00 x 2.87 in.	200, 225, 271
1966	I-6	200-cu.in.	3.68 x 3.13 in.	120
1966	V-8	289-cu.in.	4.00 x 2.87 in.	200, 225, 271
1967	I-6	200-cu.in.	3.68 x 3.13 in.	120
1967	V-8	289-cu.in.	4.00 x 2.87 in.	200, 225, 271
1967	V-8	390-cu.in.	4.05 x 3.78 in.	320
1968	I-6	200-cu.in.	3.68 x 3.13 in.	120
1968	V-8	289-cu.in.	4.00 x 2.87 in.	195
1968	V-8	302-cu.in.	4.00 x 3.00 in.	210, 230
1968	V-8	390-cu.in.	4.05 x 3.78 in.	325
1968	V-8	427-cu.in.	4.23 x 3.78 in.	390
1968	V-8	428-cu.in.	4.13 x 3.98 in.	335
1969	I-6	200-cu.in.	3.68 x 3.13 in.	115
1969	I-6	250-cu.in.	3.68 x 3.91 in.	155
1969	V-8	302-cu.in.	4.00 x 3.00 in.	220, 230, 290
1969	V-8	351-cu.in.	4.00 x 3.50 in.	250, 290
1969	V-8	390-cu.in.	4.05 x 3.78 in.	320
1969	V-8	428-cu.in.	4.13 x 3.98 in.	335
1969	V-8	429-cu.in.	4.36 x 3.59 in.	375
1970	I-6	200-cu.in.	3.68 x 3.13 in.	120
1970	I-6	250-cu.in.	3.68 x 3.91 in.	155
1970	V-8	302-cu.in.	4.00 x 3.00 in.	220, 290
1970	V-8	351-cu.in.	4.00 x 3.50 in.	250, 300
1970	V-8	428-cu.in.	4.13 x 3.98 in.	335
1970	V-8	429-cu.in.	4.36 x 3.59 in.	375
1971	I-6	250-cu.in.	3.68 x 3.91 in.	145
1971	V-8	302-cu.in.	4.00 x 3.00 in.	210
1971	V-8	351-cu.in.	4.00 x 3.50 in.	240, 280, 285, 330
1971	V-8	429-cu.in.	4.36 x 3.59 in.	370, 375

Net horsepower ratings from 1972 on.

Year	Cylinders	Displacement	Bore x Stroke	Output (Gross HP)
1972	I-6	250-cu.in.	3.68 x 3.91 in.	98
1972	V-8	302-cu.in.	4.00 x 3.00 in.	140
1972	V-8	351-cu.in.	4.00 x 3.50 in.	177, 266, 275
1973	I-6	250-cu.in.	3.68 x 3.91 in.	99
1973	V-8	302-cu.in.	4.00 x 3.00 in.	141
1973	V-8	351-cu.in.	4.00 x 3.50 in.	177, 266
1974	I-4	140-cu.in.	3.78 x 3.13 in.	85
1974	V-6	171-cu.in.	3.66 x 2.70 in.	105
1975	I-4	140-cu.in.	3.78 x 3.12 in.	83
1975	V-6	171-cu.in.	3.66 x 2.70 in.	97
1975	V-8	302-cu.in.	4.00 x 3.00 in.	122
1976	I-4	140-cu.in.	3.78 x 3.13 in.	92
1976	V-6	171-cu.in.	3.66 x 2.70 in.	103
1976	V-8	302-cu.in.	4.00 x 3.00 in.	134
1977	I-4	140-cu.in.	3.78 x 3.13 in.	89
1977	V-6	171-cu.in.	3.66 x 2.70 in.	93
1977	V-8	302-cu.in.	4.00 x 3.00 in.	139
1978	I-4	140-cu.in.	3.78 x 3.13 in.	88
1978	V-6	171-cu.in.	3.66 x 2.70 in.	90
1978	V-8	302-cu.in.	4.00 x 3.00 in.	139

Model Year Production 1964 ½-1978

Year	Production
1964½	121,538
1965	559,451
1966	607,568
1967	472,121
1968	317,404
1969	299,824
1970	190,727
1971	149,678
1972	125,093
1973	134,867
1974	385,993
1975	188,575
1976	187,567
1977	153,173
1978	192,410